OFFICIAL TOURIS

Budget Places to Stay – Cities

Information at your fingertips

This pocket guide is aimed at consumers looking for quality-rated accommodation in English cities, with room rates priced at or below £49 per night. You will find a selection of hotels, B&Bs, campus accommodation and hostels in England, with room rates of £49 or below per room per night for a double room, or £25 or below per person per night for a single room.

Star ratings

Establishments are awarded a rating of one to five stars based on a combination of quality of facilities and services provided. The more stars, the higher the quality and the greater the range of facilities and level of service.

The process to arrive at a star rating is very thorough to ensure that when you book accommodation you can be confident it will meet your expectations. Enjoy England professional assessors visit establishments annually and work to strict criteria to rate the available facilities and service.

A quality score is awarded for every aspect of the experience. For hotels and B&B accommodation this includes the comfort of the bed, the quality of the breakfast and dinner and, most importantly, the cleanliness. For self-catering properties the assessors also take into consideration the layout and design of the accommodation, the ease of use of all appliances, the range and quality of the kitchen equipment, and the variety and presentation of the visitor information provided. The warmth of welcome and the level of care that each establishment offers its guests are noted, and places that go the extra mile to make every stay a special one will be rewarded with high scores for quality.

All the national assessing bodies (VisitBritain, VisitScotland, Visit Wales and the AA*) now operate to a common set of standards for rating each category of accommodation, giving holidaymakers and travellers a clear guide on exactly what to expect at each level. An explanation of the star ratings is given below:

Ratings made easy

★	Simple, practical, no frills
★★	Well presented and well run
★★★	Good level of quality and comfort
★★★★	Excellent standard throughout
★★★★★	Exceptional with a degree of luxury

For full details of Enjoy England's Quality assessment schemes go online at **enjoyengland.com/quality**

Awaiting confirmation of rating

At the time of going to press some establishments featured in this guide had not yet been assessed for their rating for the year 2007 and so their new rating could not be included. Rating Applied For indicates this.

** The AA does not assess self-catering properties.*

Gold and Silver Awards

The Enjoy England awards are highly prized by proprietors and are only given to hotels and bed and breakfast accommodation offering the highest level of quality within their star rating, particularly in areas of housekeeping, service and hospitality, bedrooms, bathrooms and food.

National Accessible Scheme

Establishments with a National Accessible Scheme rating provide access and facilities for guests with special visual, hearing and mobility needs.

Designators explained

Hotel	A minimum of six bedrooms, but more likely to have more than 20.
Guest Accommodation	Encompassing a wide range of establishments from one room B&Bs to larger properties which may offer dinner and hold an alcohol licence.
B&B	Accommodating no more than six people, the owners of these establishments welcome you into their own home as a special guest.
Guest House	Generally comprising more than three rooms. Dinner is unlikely to be available (if it is, it will need to be booked in advance). May be licensed.
Farmhouse	B&B, and sometimes dinner, but always on a farm.
Inn	Pub with rooms, and many with restaurants, too.
Hostel	Safe, budget-priced, short-term accommodation for individuals and groups.
Campus	Accommodation provided by educational establishments including university halls of residence and student village complexes.

How to use this guide

Each accommodation entry contains information that proprietors provide regional tourist partners (except for ratings and awards).

1 2 3 4 5

DURHAM

Hamsteels Hall ★★★★Farmhouse

Hamsteels Lane, Quebec, Durham, DH7 9RS SILVER AWARD

T:	+44 (0) 1207 520388
E:	june@hamsteelshall.co.uk
W:	hamsteelshall.co.uk
Bedrooms:	5
Prices:	£40.00-£50.00 per double room per night, breakfast included Cheques/cash accepted
Open:	Seasonal opening
Description:	Serviced accommodation in an historical building with four-poster beds, en suite facilities and panoramic views. Ideal for country walks, cycling or touring. Only 10 minutes' drive from Durham City and 15 minutes' drive from Beamish.
Facilities:	Rooms: General: P Leisure:

6 7 8 9 10

1	City
2	Establishment name
3	Establishment address (or booking address if self catering)
4	Enjoy England Quality star rating and designator
5	Gold or Silver Award where applicable
6	Telephone, email and website address – note that web addresses are shown without the prefix www.
7	Accommodation details, prices and details of when establishment is open
8	At-a-glance facility symbols (for key see facing page)
9	Accessible rating where applicable
10	Cyclists/Walkers Welcome where applicable

Please note that sample entry is for illustration purposes only.
Not all symbols shown will apply to this establishment.

Key to symbols

Rooms

- Non-smoking rooms available
- Microwave
- Tea/coffee facilities in all bedrooms
- Phone in all bedrooms
- Cots available
- Central heating
- Colour TV
- DVD player
- Compact disc player
- Four-poster bed available
- Bedrooms on ground floor
- Air conditioning
- Freezer
- Dishwasher
- Hairdryer in all bedrooms
- Internet

General

- Non-smoking establishment
- Night porter
- Parking on site
- Public phone
- Open fire(s)
- Children welcome (check with accommodation for minimum age)
- Highchairs
- Licensed bar
- Coach parties welcome
- Restaurant
- Shop on site
- Evening entertainment
- Garden/patio
- Pets welcome
- Lounge
- Washing machine or laundry facilities
- Ironing facilities
- Lift

Leisure

- Sauna
- Swimming pool – outdoor
- Swimming pool – indoor
- Whirlpool
- Riding/pony trekking nearby
- Tennis court(s)
- Games room
- Fishing nearby
- Golf nearby
- Cycle hire nearby
- Gym/fitness room

Mobility Symbols

Typically suitable for a person with sufficient mobility to climb a flight of steps but who would benefit from fixtures and fittings to aid balance.

Typically suitable for a person with restricted walking ability and for those who may need to use a wheelchair some of the time and can negotiate a maximum of three steps.

Typically suitable for a person who depends on the use of a wheelchair and transfers to and from the wheelchair in a seated position. This person may be an independent traveller.

Typically suitable for a person who depends on the use of a wheelchair in a seated position. This person also requires personal/mechanical assistance to aid transfer (eg carer, hoist).

Visual Impairment Symbols

Typically provides key additional services and facilities to meet the needs of visually impaired guests.

Typically provides a higher level of additional services and facilities to meet the needs of visually impaired guests.

Hearing Impairment Symbols

Typically provides key additional services and facilities to meet the needs of guests with a hearing impairment.

Typically provides a higher level of additional services and facilities to meet the needs of guests with a hearing impairment.

Cyclists Welcome and Walkers Welcome

Participants actively encourage cycling and walking by providing clean up areas for washing or drying off, help with special meal arrangements, maps and books to look up for cycling and walking routes.

BATH

Abbey Farm

★★★★Farmhouse

Camerton Hill, Camerton, Bath, BA2 0PS

T:	+44 (0) 1761 471640
Bedrooms:	3
Prices:	£25.00-£55.00 per double room per night, breakfast included
Open:	Year round except Christmas and New Year
Description:	Sample the warm hospitality of this family-run listed farmhouse, one mile off the A367.
Facilities:	Rooms: General: Leisure:

BATH

Aquae Sulis

♦♦♦♦Guest Accommodation

174/176 Newbridge Road, Bath, BA1 3LE

T: **E:** **W:**	+44 (0) 1225 420061 enquiries@aquaesulishotel.co.uk aquaesulishotel.co.uk
Bedrooms:	13
Prices:	£45.00-£95.00 per double room per night, breakfast included Debit/credit card, cheques/cash accepted
Open:	Seasonal opening – contact for details
Description:	Conveniently situated Victorian hotel retaining period features yet modernised for the 21stC guest. Well appointed, non-smoking bedrooms, all en suite. Bar, evening meal available, garden and ample parking.
Facilities:	Rooms: General: Leisure:

BATH

Ashgrove Guesthouse

★★★★B&B

39 Bathwick Street, Bath, BA2 6PA

T:	+44 (0) 1225 421911
Bedrooms:	9
Prices:	£40.00-£50.00 per double room per night, breakfast included Debit/credit card, cheques/cash accepted
Open:	Year round except Christmas and New Year
Description:	Ashgrove is a Georgian Grade II Listed building built by Thomas Baldwin in c1750. A friendly, family-run guesthouse at the very most, six minutes' level walk and you are in the main city centre and in reach of Bath's many attractions.
Facilities:	Rooms: General:

BATH

Athole Guesthouse

★★★★★B&B
GOLD AWARD

33 Upper Oldfield Park, Bath, BA2 3JX

T: +44 (0) 1225 320000
E: info@atholehouse.co.uk
W: atholehouse.co.uk

Bedrooms: 4

Prices: £48.00-£78.00 per double room per night, breakfast included
Debit/credit card, cheques/cash, euros accepted

Open: Year round except Christmas and New Year

Description: A large Victorian home with quiet bedrooms and sparkling bathrooms.

Facilities: Rooms:
General:
Leisure:

BATH

Bath YHA

★★★Hostel

Bathwick Hill, Bath, BA2 6JZ

T: +44 (0) 1225 465674
E: bath@yha.org.uk
W: yha.org.uk

Bedrooms: 27

Prices: £9.00-£68.00 per person per night, room only
Debit/credit card, cheques/cash accepted

Open: Year round

Description: Youth hostel occupying a handsome, Italian-style mansion set in large grounds overlooking the historic city of Bath.

Facilities: Rooms:
General:

BATH

Bridgnorth House

★★★B&B

2 Crescent Gardens, Bath, BA1 2NA

T: +44 (0) 1225 331186

Bedrooms: 4

Prices: £42.00-£55.00 per double room per night, breakfast included
Cheques/cash accepted

Open: Year round except Christmas and New Year

Description: Bridgnorth House is an elegant townhouse two minutes from the Royal Crescent in Bath. It is beautifully decorated and visitors mostly come from recommendation or repeat business.

Facilities: Rooms:
General:

BATH

Cherry Tree Villa
♦♦♦Guest Accommodation

7 Newbridge Hill, Bath, BA1 3PW

T: +44 (0) 1225 331671
E: cherrytreebath@hotmail.co.uk
W: visitbath.co.uk

Bedrooms: 4

Prices: £40.00-£50.00 per double room per night, breakfast included
Cheques/cash accepted

Open: Year round except Christmas

Description: Modernised, Victorian house tastefully decorated. Friendly atmosphere. Situated within easy walking distance of city centre through pleasant park.

Facilities: Rooms:
General: **P**

BATH

Flaxley Villa
★★★B&B

9 Newbridge Hill, Bath, BA1 3PW

T: +44 (0) 1225 313237
E: flaxleyvilla@fsmail.net

Bedrooms: 3

Prices: £45.00-£65.00 per double room per night, breakfast included

Open: Year round

Description: A comfortable Victorian house within easy reach of Royal Crescent and main attractions, and a few minutes by car to city centre.

Facilities: Rooms:
General: **P**
Leisure:

BATH

Glan Y Dwr
♦♦♦Guest Accommodation

14 Newbridge Hill, Bath, BA1 3PU

T: +44 (0) 1225 317521
E: glanydwr@hotmail.com
W: glanydwr.co.uk

Bedrooms: 5

Prices: £40.00-£60.00 per double room per night, breakfast included
Cheques/cash accepted

Open: Year round

Description: A small, family-run business set in a large Victorian house within walking distance of Bath city centre on frequent bus route.

Facilities: Rooms:
General: **P**

BATH

Radnor Guesthouse

★★★★Guesthouse

9 Pulteney Terrace, Pulteney Road, Bath, BA2 4HJ

T:	+44 (0) 1225 316159
E:	info@radnorguesthouse.co.uk
W:	radnorguesthouse.co.uk
Bedrooms:	5
Prices:	£48.00-£60.00 per double room per night, breakfast included Cheques/cash accepted
Open:	Seasonal opening – closed Christmas
Description:	Comfortable en suite accommodation with full central heating. English breakfast. Situated a few minutes from city centre. Full fire certificate.
Facilities:	Rooms: General:

BATH

The Firs

★★★★B&B

2 Newbridge Hill, Bath, BA1 3PU

T:	+44 (0) 1225 334575
Bedrooms:	3
Prices:	£40.00-£55.00 per double room per night, breakfast included
Open:	Year round
Description:	Victorian B&B, newly renovated to a high standard. Parking, non-smoking, friendly family home. Single rate for double room £40 per night.
Facilities:	Rooms: General:

BRADFORD-ON-AVON

Conifers

★★B&B

4 King Alfred Way, Winsley, Bradford-on-Avon, Wiltshire, BA15 2NG

T:	+44 (0) 1225 722482
Bedrooms:	2
Prices:	£44.00-£50.00 per double room per night, breakfast included Cheques/cash accepted
Open:	Year round
Description:	Semi-detached house, 2.25 miles from Bradford-on-Avon, seven miles from Bath. Quiet area, pleasant outlook. Friendly atmosphere. Off-road parking. On bus route, a lovely garden. Recommended pub evening meal.
Facilities:	Rooms: General:

BRADFORD-ON-AVON

Great Ashley Farm ♦♦♦♦Guest Accommodation

Great Ashley, Bradford-on-Avon, BA15 2PP GOLD AWARD

T: +44 (0) 1225 864563
E: info@greatashley.co.uk
W: greatashley.co.uk

Bedrooms: 2

Prices: £45.00-£65.00 per double room per night, breakfast included

Open: Year round

Description: Working farm with delightful farmhouse, lovely en suite rooms, great hospitality, delicious breakfast; secluded yet convenient from Bath/M4; golf course nearby. Gold award for quality and service and Taste of the West Food and Drink Bronze award.

Facilities: Rooms:
General:
Leisure:

BRADFORD-ON-AVON

Springfields ♦♦♦♦Guest Accommodation

Great Ashley, Bradford-on-Avon, BA15 2PP

T: +44 (0) 1225 866125
E: christine.rawlings@farmersweekly.net
W: bed-and-breakfast.org

Bedrooms: 1

Prices: £45.00-£50.00 per double room per night, breakfast included

Open: Year round except Christmas and New Year

Description: Unique, ground level en suite double room with adjoining lounge/dining room. Peaceful countryside setting, with easy access to Bath.

Facilities: Rooms:
General:
Leisure:

BRISTOL

Ferndale Guesthouse ♦♦♦Guest Accommodation

37 Deanery Road, Kingswood, Bristol, BS15 9JB

T: +44 (0) 117 985 8247

Bedrooms: 8

Prices: £45.00 per double room per night, breakfast included
Debit/credit card, euros accepted

Open: Year round

Description: Located on the Bristol Ring Road A420. Easy access to cycle track. Easy access to Bath or Bristol.

Facilities: Rooms:
General:

BRISTOL

Greenacres (Stanton Wick) ★★Guest Accommodation

Stanton Wick, Bristol, BS39 4BX

T:	+44 (0) 1761 490397
Bedrooms:	6
Prices:	£48.00-£90.00 per double room per night, breakfast included
Open:	Seasonal opening – contact for details
Description:	A friendly welcome awaits in peaceful setting, off A37. Relax and enjoy panoramic views across Chew Valley to Dundry Hills.
Facilities:	Rooms: General: P Leisure:

BATH

Kingston House B&B ♦♦Guest Accommodation

101 Hardenhuish Road, Brislington, Bristol, BS4 3SR

T:	+44 (0) 117 9712 45607921770827
Bedrooms:	3
Prices:	£46.00-£50.00 per double room per night, breakfast included
Open:	Seasonal opening – contact for details
Description:	Very smart and tidy rooms, complemented by excellent service, hearty breakfast and a friendly ambience.
Facilities:	Call for details.

CORSHAM

Church Farm ♦♦♦♦Guest Accommodation

Hartham, Corsham, Wiltshire, SN13 0PU

T:	+44 (0) 1249 715180
E:	churchfarmbandb@hotmail.com
W:	churchfarm.cjb.net
Bedrooms:	4
Prices:	£30.00-£40.00 per person per night, breakfast included Cheques/cash accepted
Open:	Seasonal opening – contact for details
Description:	Cotswold farmhouse and adjacent barn accommodation, offering wonderful views over farm and parkland. Good base for visiting Bath, Castle Combe and Lacock.
Facilities:	Rooms: General: P

CORSHAM

Saltbox Farm

★★★★Farmhouse

Box, Corsham, Wiltshire, SN13 8PT

T:	+44 (0) 1225 742608
E:	bbsaltboxfarm@yahoo.co.uk
W:	saltboxfarm.verypretty.co.uk
Bedrooms:	2
Prices:	£46.00-£52.00 per double room per night, breakfast included Cheques/cash accepted
Open:	Seasonal opening – contact for details
Description:	Listed 18thC farmhouse nestled beneath the Cotswolds in the peaceful setting of the Box Valley, six miles north-east of Bath.
Facilities:	Rooms: General: P Leisure:

FROME

Eden Vale Farm

★★★Farmhouse

Mill Lane, Beckington, Frome, Somerset, BA11 6SN

T:	+44 (0) 1373 830371
E:	bandb@edenvalefarm.co.uk
W:	edenvalefarm.co.uk
Bedrooms:	3
Prices:	£45.00-£50.00 per double room per night, room only Cheques/cash accepted
Open:	Year round Closed New Year
Description:	Farmhouse dating back to Doomsday, was originally a corn mill. Secluded, riverside setting 10 miles from Bath, 0.75 miles from Beckington village.
Facilities:	Rooms: TV General: P Leisure: U

MELKSHAM

Church Farm

★★★★Farmhouse

Church Street, Atworth, Melksham, Wiltshire, SN12 8JA

T:	+44 (0) 1225 702215
E:	churchfarm@tinyonline.co.uk
W:	churchfarm-atworth.freeserve.co.uk
Bedrooms:	2
Prices:	£45.00-£60.00 per double room per night, breakfast included Cheques/cash accepted
Open:	Seasonal opening – contact for details
Description:	Grade II Listed building with large garden situated on the edge of village. Working dairy farm. Tithe barn.
Facilities:	Rooms: TV General: P Leisure:

TROWBRIDGE

49a Church Lane ♦♦♦♦Guest Accommodation

North Bradley, Trowbridge, Wiltshire, BA14 0TA SILVER AWARD

T: +44 (0) 1225 762558
E: m-wise@amserve.com

Bedrooms: 3

Prices: £32.00-£50.00 per double room per night, breakfast included

Open: Year round except Christmas

Description: Large roomy house with beautiful garden and overlooking Westbury white horse and hills, 1.5 miles from Trowbridge in a quiet village.

Facilities: Rooms:
General: P

TROWBRIDGE

Lion and Fiddle ♦♦♦Guest Accommodation

Devizes Road, Hilperton, Trowbridge, Wiltshire, BA14 7QS

T: +44 (0) 1225 776392

Bedrooms: 5

Prices: £55.00 per double room per night, breakfast included
Debit/credit card, cheques/cash, euros accepted

Open: Year round except Christmas and New Year

Description: A well-known local coaching inn on outskirts of county town, providing excellent food and drink and B&B en suite accommodation, in a friendly atmosphere.

Facilities: Rooms:
General: P
Leisure:

TROWBRIDGE

Sue's B & B ★★★Guest Accommodation

25 Blair Road, Trowbridge, Wiltshire, BA14 9JZ

T: +44 (0) 1225 764559
E: sue_b_n_b@yahoo.com
W: visitbritain.com

Bedrooms: 3

Prices: £40.00 per double room per night, breakfast included

Open: Year round except Christmas

Description: Pleasant, extended, small, friendly, family-run house on quiet estate 12 miles from Bath. Close to records office and sports centre.

Facilities: Rooms:
General: P
Leisure:

BIRMINGHAM

Alden ♦♦♦Guest Accommodation

7 Elmdon Road, Marston Green, Birmingham, B37 7BS

T: +44 (0) 121 779 2063

Bedrooms: 3

Prices: £35.00-£45.00 per double room per night, breakfast included

Open: Year round except Christmas and New Year

Description: Family B&B, home comforts, friendly.

Facilities: Rooms:
General: P

BIRMINGHAM

Elmdon Guesthouse ♦♦♦Guest Accommodation

2369 Coventry Road, Sheldon, Birmingham, B26 3PN

T: +44 (0) 121 688 1720
E: elmdonhouse@blueyonder.co.uk
W: elmdonguesthouse.com

Bedrooms: 7

Prices: £48.00-£60.00 per double room per night, breakfast included
Debit/credit card, cheques/cash, euros accepted

Open: Year round

Description: Family-run guesthouse. B&B, en suite facilities. Television in all rooms including Sky. On main A45 close to the National Exhibition Centre, airport, railway and city centre.

Facilities: Rooms:
General: P

BIRMINGHAM

Rollason Wood Hotel ♦♦Guest Accommodation

130 Wood End Road, Erdington, Birmingham, B24 8BJ

T: +44 (0) 121 373 1230
E: rollwood@globalnet.co.uk
W: rollasonwoodhotel.co.uk

Bedrooms: 35

Prices: £36.00-£49.50 per double room per night, breakfast included
Debit/credit card, cheques/cash accepted

Open: Year round except Christmas and New Year

Description: Family-run hotel one mile from M6 exit 6. Accommodation includes budget rooms as well as those with private bathrooms.

Facilities: Rooms:
General: P
Leisure:

COVENTRY

Blythe Paddocks

★★★Guest Accommodation

Barston Lane, Coventry, CV7 7BT

T:	+44 (0) 1676 533050
Bedrooms:	5
Prices:	£46.00-£54.00 per double room per night, breakfast included
Open:	Year round except Christmas and New Year
Description:	Country residence home standing in five acres. Ten minutes' from Birmingham Airport and the National Exhibition Centre. National Agricultural Centre at Stoneleigh is eight miles.
Facilities:	Rooms: General: P

SOLIHULL

1 Blythe Way

★★★★Guest Accommodation

1 Blythe Way, Solihull, B91 3EY

T:	+44 (0) 121 711 1070
E:	deecooper@blueyonder.co.uk
Bedrooms:	2
Prices:	£48.00 per double room per night, breakfast included
Open:	Year round except Christmas and New Year
Description:	Situated in a secluded, tree-lined cul-de-sac, this lovely detached home offers first class en suite accommodation.
Facilities:	Rooms: General: P

SOLIHULL

Baltimore House

★★B&B

12 Brampton Crescent, Shirley, Solihull, B90 3SY

T:	+44 (0) 121 744 9100
E:	egeeborall@aol.com
Bedrooms:	2
Prices:	£35.00 per double room per night, breakfast included
Open:	Year round
Description:	B&B in a quiet cul-de-sac overlooking Robin Hood golf course, comfortable rooms, new bath/shower room for guests.
Facilities:	Rooms: TV General: P Leisure:

SOLIHULL

Ravenhurst

♦♦♦Guest Accommodation

56 Lode Lane, Solihull, B91 2AW

T:	+44 (0) 121 705 5754
E:	ravenhurstaccom@aol.com
W:	ravenhurst-guesthouse.co.uk
Bedrooms:	4
Prices:	£45.00-£80.00 per double room per night, breakfast included Debit/credit card, cheques/cash, euros accepted
Open:	Year round
Description:	Magnificent Victorian guesthouse established for 15 years, in Solihull centre with numerous facilities and five minutes from NEC and airport.
Facilities:	Rooms: General: P

BRADFORD

Ivy Guesthouse

♦♦Guest Accommodation

3 Melbourne Place, Bradford, BD5 0HZ

T:	+44 (0) 1274 727060
E:	NickBaggio@aol.com
W:	ivyguesthousebradford.com
Bedrooms:	10
Prices:	£36.00 per double room per night, breakfast included
Open:	Year round
Description:	Large, detached, Listed house built of Yorkshire stone. Car park and gardens. Near university, museums and city centre.
Facilities:	Rooms: General: P

BRADFORD

New Beehive Inn

★★Guest Accommodation

171 Westgate, Bradford, BD1 3AA

T:	+44 (0) 1274 721784
E:	newbeehive@talk21.com
W:	s-h-systems.co.uk/hotels/beehive.html
Bedrooms:	8
Prices:	£42.00 per double room per night, room only
Open:	Year round
Description:	Edwardian, gas-lit inn. About 0.5 miles to the city centre and close to major attractions.
Facilities:	Rooms: General: P Leisure:

BRADFORD

Norland Guesthouse ★★★Guest Accommodation

695 Great Horton Road, Bradford, BD7 4DU

T:	+44 (0) 1274 571698
E:	norlandhouse@hotmail.co.uk
W:	norlandguesthouse.gbr.cc
Bedrooms:	9
Prices:	£35.00-£40.00 per double room per night, breakfast included
Open:	Year round
Description:	Norland guesthouse is a family-run guesthouse in a detached Victorian residence in Bradford. In quiet, pleasant surroundings, 1.5 miles from the city centre, National Film and Photography Museum, the Alhambra Theatre and Bradford ice rink.
Facilities:	Rooms: General: P

BRIGHOUSE

Waterfront Lodge ★★Hotel

Huddersfield Road, Brighouse, HD6 1JZ

T:	+44 (0) 1484 715566
E:	info@waterfrontlodge.co.uk
W:	waterfrontlodge.co.uk
Bedrooms:	42
Prices:	£40.00-£90.00 per double room per night, room only Debit/credit card accepted
Open:	Seasonal opening – contact for details
Description:	Quality designer accommodation at a realistic price.
Facilities:	Rooms: General: P

HALIFAX

Joan's Guesthouse ♦♦♦Guest Accommodation

13 Heath Park Avenue, Halifax, HX1 2PP

T:	+44 (0) 1422 369290
Bedrooms:	2
Prices:	£22.50-£22.50 per family room per night, breakfast included
Open:	Seasonal opening – contact for details
Description:	Large Victorian terrace property situated close to the town centre and Eureka Museum.
Facilities:	Rooms: General: P

HALIFAX

Ploughcroft Cottage ★★★Guest Accommodation

53 Ploughcroft Lane, Halifax, HX3 6TX

T:	+44 (0) 1422 341205
E:	ploughcroft.cottage@Care4free.net
W:	ploughcroftcottage.com
Bedrooms:	4
Prices:	£39.00-£45.00 per double room per night, breakfast included
Open:	Seasonal opening – contact for details
Description:	Ploughcroft Cottage is set in a unique rural position with magnificent views over the town and surrounding countryside. Halifax offers a unique Victorian heritage of architectural acclaim and is only five minutes away by car.
Facilities:	Rooms: General:

HALIFAX

Rockcliffe West ★★★★B&B

Burnley Road, Luddendenfoot, Halifax, HX2 6HL

T:	+44 (0) 1422 882151
E:	rockcliffe.b.b@virgin.net
W:	rockcliffewest.co.uk
Bedrooms:	2
Prices:	£42.00-£45.00 per double room per night, breakfast included
Open:	Seasonal opening – contact for details
Description:	Delightful 19thC home set amid beautiful private gardens. Friendly atmosphere.
Facilities:	Rooms: General: P Leisure:

HALIFAX

Rook Residence ♦♦♦Guest Accommodation

69 Shelf Hall Lane, Shelf, Halifax, HX3 7LT

T:	+44 (0) 1274 601586
E:	rookbnb@btinternet.com
W:	bnb.com
Bedrooms:	7
Prices:	£40.00-£44.00 per double room per night, breakfast included
Open:	Year round
Description:	Rook Residence is a B&B establishment located in Halifax. A comfortable, clean and friendly place to stay for hikers, cyclists, tourists and business people alike. You are welcome.
Facilities:	Rooms: General: P

HALIFAX

Travis House
★★★Guest Accommodation

8 West Parade, Halifax, HX1 2TA

T:	+44 (0) 1422 365727
Bedrooms:	3
Prices:	£40.00 per double room per night, breakfast included
Open:	Year round
Description:	Friendly, family-run B&B accommodation offering comfort and quality to all our guests. Five minutes to town centre.
Facilities:	Rooms: General: P

HALIFAX

Whitehill Lodge
♦♦♦Guest Accommodation

102 Keighley Road, Halifax, HX2 8HF

T: **E:**	+44 (0) 1422 240813 keithmac102@aol.com
Bedrooms:	3
Prices:	£40.00-£50.00 per double room per night, breakfast included
Open:	Year round
Description:	Whitehill Lodge is a guesthouse establishment located in Halifax.
Facilities:	Rooms: General: P

HUDDERSFIELD

Cambridge Lodge
♦♦♦Guest Accommodation

4 Clare Hill, Huddersfield, HD1 5BS

T: **E:** **W:**	+44 (0) 1484 519892 cambridge.lodge.hudd@btconnect.com cambridgelodge.co.uk
Bedrooms:	34
Prices:	£45.00 per double room per night, breakfast included
Open:	Year round
Description:	We have 34 en suite bedrooms, all rooms with tea-/coffee-making facilities, telephone and colour TV in all rooms. Ample free parking and CCTV coverage.
Facilities:	Rooms: General: P

HUDDERSFIELD

Croppers Arms ★★★★Guest Accommodation

136 Westbourne Road, Huddersfield, HD1 4LF

T:	+44 (0) 1484 421522
E:	da@ytb.org.uk
Bedrooms:	6
Prices:	£49.50 per double room per night, breakfast included
Open:	Year round
Description:	Croppers Arms is a friendly public house a mile from Huddersfield town centre. Six en suite rooms furnished with emphasis on standards.
Facilities:	Rooms: [symbols] General: [symbols]

HUDDERSFIELD

Holmcliffe Guesthouse ★★★★Guesthouse

16 Mountjoy Road, Edgerton, Huddersfield, HD1 5PZ

T:	+44 (0) 1484 429598
E:	j.wilcockson1@ntlworld.com
Bedrooms:	8
Prices:	£22.50-£25.00 per double room per night, breakfast included
Open:	Seasonal opening – contact for details
Description:	Holmcliffe guesthouse offers comfortable accommodation in a quiet residential area close to town. Close to east- and west-bound M62. Hospitality award winner. Holmcliffe has the added advantage of a non-smoking environment.
Facilities:	Rooms: [symbols] General: [symbols]

HUDDERSFIELD

Premier Travel Inn ♦♦Guest Accommodation

Wakefield Road, Brighouse, Huddersfield, West Yorkshire, HD6 4HA

T:	+44 (0) 870 990 6360
W:	premiertravelinn.com/pti/visitbritain.do?hotelid=HUDOLD
Bedrooms:	3
Prices:	£40.00 per twin room per night, breakfast included
Open:	Year round
Description:	Premier Travel Inn is the UK's leading value hotel chain. We guarantee clean, comfortable rooms and a friendly and efficient service – everything you need for a good night's sleep.
Facilities:	Rooms: [symbols] General: [symbols]

ILKLEY

Chevin End Guesthouse

★★★Guesthouse

West Chevin Road, Menston, Ilkley, LS29 6BE

T: +44 (0) 1943 876845
E: enquiries@chevinendguesthouse.co.uk
W: chevinendguesthouse.co.uk

Bedrooms: 8

Prices: £45.00 per double room per night, breakfast included

Open: Year round

Description: Chevin End guesthouse is a B&B eight-bedroomed barn conversion adjoining Chevin End Farm. Set in a rural location it has panoramic Wharfe Valley views.

Facilities: Rooms:
General: P

ILKLEY

Hillcrest

★★★B&B

24 Hill Crescent, Burley in Wharfedale, Ilkley, LS29 7QG

T: +44 (0) 1943 863258
E: angela@hillcrest-burley.co.uk
W: hillcrest-burley.co.uk

Bedrooms: 2

Prices: £40.00-£45.00 per double room per night, breakfast included

Open: Year round

Description: Comfortable/friendly family B&B. Private parking, colour TV, tea-/coffee-making facilities, £20 single, Double from £35.

Facilities: Rooms:
General: P

KEIGHLEY

Brontë Hotel

★★★Guest Accommodation

Lees Lane, Haworth, Keighley, BD22 8RA

T: +44 (0) 1535 644112
E: bronte-hotel@btinternet.co.uk
W: bronte-hotel.co.uk

Bedrooms: 11

Prices: £45.00-£70.00 per double room per night, breakfast included

Open: Seasonal opening – closed Christmas

Description: The Parsonage is the former home of the Brontë family. Situated on the edge of the moors, five minutes' walk from the station.

Facilities: Rooms:
General: P

KEIGHLEY

The Apothecary Guesthouse ★★Guesthouse

86 Main Street, Haworth, Keighley, BD22 8DP

T: +44 (0) 1535 643642
E: Sisleyd@aol.com
W: theapothecaryguesthouse.co.uk

Bedrooms: 8

Prices: £40.00-£50.00 per double room per night, breakfast included
Debit/credit card accepted

Open: Year round

Description: At the top of the main street, opposite the famous Brontë church and a minute from the Brontë Parsonage and moors.

Facilities: Rooms:
General: P
Leisure:

LEEDS

Adriatic Hotel ★★★Guest Accommodation

87 Harehills Avenue, Leeds, LS8 4ET

T: +44 (0) 113 262 0115
E: adriatichotel@btconnect.com
W: theadriatichotel.co.uk

Bedrooms: 26

Prices: £48.00-£65.00 per double room per night, breakfast included

Open: Year round

Description: Privately-run budget hotel minutes from city and walking distance to St James Hospital. All rooms en suite, car parking, restaurant, lounge, bar.

Facilities: Rooms:
General: P

LEEDS

Avalon Guesthouse ★★★Guesthouse

132 Woodsley Road, Leeds, LS2 9LZ

T: +44 (0) 113 243 2545
E: da@ytb.org.uk
W: avalonguesthouseleeds.co.uk

Bedrooms: 10

Prices: £45.00-£50.00 per double room per night, breakfast included
Debit/credit card accepted

Open: Year round

Description: Superbly decorated Victorian establishment close to the university, Leeds General Infirmary and less than a mile from the city centre.

Facilities: Rooms:
General: P

LEEDS

Bridge Farm Hotel ♦♦♦Guest Accommodation

Wakefield Road, Swillington, Leeds, LS26 8PZ

T: +44 (0) 113 282 3718
E: bridgefarm.hotel@btinternet.com

Bedrooms: 13

Prices: £45.00-£49.50 per double room per night, breakfast included

Open: Seasonal opening – contact for details

Description: Tastefully-converted and centrally-heated, 18thC coaching house, with easy access to the M62, M1 and A1. Ten minutes from city centre.

Facilities: Rooms:
General: P
Leisure:

LEEDS

End Lea ★★★★Guesthouse

39 Town Street, Gildersome, Leeds, LS27 7AX

T: +44 (0) 113 252 1661
E: patricia.mcbride@homecall.co.uk

Bedrooms: 4

Prices: £45.00 per double room per night, breakfast included

Open: Year round

Description: End Lea is friendly, family-run guesthouse near city centre and football ground. Quality detached building, good gardens and secure parking. Very good decor and furniture throughout. Close to M62, M621 and M1.

Facilities: Rooms:
General: P

LEEDS

Glengarth Hotel ♦♦♦Guest Accommodation

162 Woodsley Road, Leeds, LS2 9LZ

T: +44 (0) 113 245 7940

Bedrooms: 14

Prices: £40.00-£50.00 per double room per night, breakfast included
Debit/credit card accepted

Open: Year round

Description: Glengarth Hotel is a friendly, family hotel near the university, infirmary hospital and within a mile of the city centre. With easy access to the M1/M62.

Facilities: Rooms:
General: P

LEEDS

Green House ♦♦♦Guest Accommodation

5 Bank View Terrace, Leeds, LS7 2EX

T:	+44 (0) 113 268 1380
Bedrooms:	3
Prices:	£45.00-£55.00 per double room per night, breakfast included
Open:	Year round
Description:	Green House is a Victorian guesthouse with a welcoming decor inspired by designer proprietor.
Facilities:	Rooms: General: P

LEEDS

Headingley Lodge Hotel ★★★Guest Accommodation

Headingley Stadium, St Michael's Lane, Headingley, Leeds, LS6 3BR

T: **E:** **W:**	+44 (0) 113 278 5323 tamsin_lee@talk21.com headingleylodge.co.uk
Bedrooms:	36
Prices:	£39.50-£49.50 per double room per night, room only
Open:	Year round
Description:	Headingley Lodge forms part of the redeveloped Headingley Stadium complex within easy reach of Leeds city centre and offers 36 spacious bedrooms with stunning views of the world famous cricket ground.
Facilities:	Rooms: General: P

LEEDS

Manxdene Private Hotel ★★Guest Accommodation

154 Woodsley Road, Leeds, LS2 9LZ

T: **E:**	+44 (0) 113 243 2586 manxdenehotel@leedscity.wanadoo.co.uk
Bedrooms:	12
Prices:	£40.00-£60.00 per double room per night, breakfast included
Open:	Seasonal opening – closed Christmas
Description:	A family-run, friendly hotel assuring a warm welcome. Convenient for universities, hospitals, city centre, shops, soccer, rugby and cricket.
Facilities:	Rooms: General:

LEEDS

Myrtle House ♦♦♦Guest Accommodation

31 Wakefield Road, Garforth, Leeds, LS25 1AN

T:	+44 (0) 113 286 6445
Bedrooms:	6
Prices:	£42.00-£46.00 per double room per night, breakfast included
Open:	Seasonal opening – contact for details
Description:	Myrtle House is a B&B located in Garforth. Spacious Victorian terraced house (a mile from Jct 47 M1). All rooms have tea-/coffee-making facilities, TV, vanity basins and central heating.
Facilities:	Rooms: General:

LEEDS

Oak Villa Hotel ★★★Guest Accommodation

55-57 Cardigan Road, Leeds, LS6 1DW

T:	+44 (0) 113 275 8439
E:	oakvillahotel@msn.com
W:	oakvillahotel.co.uk
Bedrooms:	26
Prices:	£46.00-£62.00 per double room per night, breakfast included Debit/credit card accepted
Open:	Seasonal opening – contact for details
Description:	Oak Villa is situated in the heart of a pleasant wooded conservation centre. It is a family-run hotel near to all amenities.
Facilities:	Rooms: General: P

LEEDS

St Michael's Tower Hotel ★★Guest Accommodation

5 St Michael's Villas, Cardigan Road, Leeds, LS6 3AF

T:	+44 (0) 113 275 5557
W:	leeds-headingleyhotels.com
Bedrooms:	24
Prices:	£40.00-£43.00 per double room per night, breakfast included
Open:	Seasonal opening – contact for details
Description:	Licensed, private hotel 1.5 miles from the city centre. Close to both the university and Yorkshire Cricket Ground. Warm and friendly welcome.
Facilities:	Rooms: General: P

LEEDS

The Moorlea Hotel ♦♦♦Guest Accommodation

146 Woodsley Road, Leeds, LS2 9LZ

T: +44 (0) 113 243 2653
E: themoorleahotel@aol.com

Bedrooms: 10

Prices: £44.00-£54.00 per double room per night, breakfast included

Open: Year round

Description: Family-run, warm, friendly atmosphere, comfortable accommodation 15 minutes' walk from the city centre, five minutes from University and 10 minutes from General Infirmary. Cocktail Bar with TV for relaxation!

Facilities: Rooms:
General: P
Leisure:

LEEDS

Wike Ridge Farm ♦♦♦♦Guest Accommodation

Wike Ridge Lane, Leeds, LS17 9JF

T: +44 (0) 113 266 1190

Bedrooms: 5

Prices: £48.00 per double room per night, breakfast included

Open: Year round

Description: Yorkshire farmhouse with old world charm. Founded late 18thC. Part of the Earl Harewood's estate until 1901.

Facilities: Rooms:
General:
Leisure:

PUDSEY

Heatherlea House ★★★B&B

105 Littlemoor Road, Pudsey, LS28 8AP

T: +44 (0) 113 257 4397
E: da@ytb.org.uk

Bedrooms: 2

Prices: £42.00 per double room per night, breakfast included

Open: Year round

Description: Heatherlea House has a pleasant atmosphere in tastefully furnished rooms. Large award-winning gardens, quiet surroundings. Close to city centre, motorways, airport and on bus route. Non-smoking establishment.

Facilities: Rooms:
General: P
Leisure:

SHIPLEY

Clifton Lodge Guesthouse ★★★Guest Accommodation

75 Kirkgate, Shipley, BD18 3LU

T: +44 (0) 1274 580509
E: cliftonlodge75@hotmail.com

Bedrooms: 13

Prices: £40.00 per double room per night, breakfast included
Debit/credit card accepted

Open: Seasonal opening – closed Christmas

Description: Clifton Lodge guesthouse is a B&B establishment centrally situated close to Bradford and Leeds. Bus and railway stations close by. Convenient base for touring famous landmarks such as Saltaire and Haworth.

Facilities: Rooms:
General: P
Leisure:

SHIPLEY

Ford House Farm B&B ★★★★Guest Accommodation

Ford Houses, Buck Lane, Baildon, Shipley, BD17 7RW

T: +44 (0) 1274 584489
E: fordhousefarm@hotmail.com
W: fordhousefarmbedandbreakfast.co.uk

Bedrooms: 2

Prices: £45.00-£50.00 per double room per night, breakfast included

Open: Year round

Description: Large Victorian house with beautiful views down to the River Aire. Easy access to riverbank and canal towpath for wonderful walks.

Facilities: Rooms:
General: P

SHIPLEY

Langbar House ★★★★B&B

Langbar House, 8 Temple Rhydding Drive, Baildon, Shipley, BD17 5PU

T: +44 (0) 1274 599900
E: enquiry@langbarhouse.co.uk
W: langbarhouse.co.uk

Bedrooms: 2

Prices: £40.00-£45.00 per double room per night, breakfast included

Open: Seasonal opening – contact for details

Description: Located just half a mile from Baildon village centre in West Yorkshire, Langbar House is a semi-detached house offering spacious, high-quality accommodation with off-road parking. An ideal place to base yourself for business, leisure or touring.

Facilities: Rooms:
General: P

WAKEFIELD

Foxwood
★★★★Guest Accommodation

Carr Lane, Carlton, Wakefield, WF3 3RT

T:	+44 (0) 113 282 4786
E:	da@ytb.org.uk
Bedrooms:	7
Prices:	£35.00 per double room per night, breakfast included
Open:	Year round
Description:	Foxwood guesthouse is a beautiful accommodation, set in three acres of woodland and gardens. Featuring large carp pond, home to some of the biggest fish in the country. All rooms en suite with combination video/TVs.
Facilities:	Rooms: General:

WAKEFIELD

The Bank House Hotel
★★Hotel

11 Bank Street, Westgate, Wakefield, WF1 1EH

T:	+44 (0) 1924 368248
Bedrooms:	12
Prices:	£45.00-£50.00 per double room per night, breakfast included
Open:	Year round
Description:	The Bank House Hotel is located city central with pubs, shops, restaurants and public transport a few steps away. We are a small family-run business with a warm and friendly environment. Families, contractors, parties and business stops all welcome.
Facilities:	Rooms: General: P

BRIGHTON

Ambassador Hotel
♦♦♦♦Guest Accommodation

22 New Steine, Brighton, BN2 1PD

T:	+44 (0) 1273 676869
E:	nick.head@nichotel.co.uk
W:	ambassadorbrighton.co.uk
Bedrooms:	24
Prices:	£45.00-£140.00 per double room per night, breakfast included Debit/credit card accepted
Open:	Year round
Description:	Centrally located in a Georgian garden square overlooking the sea, with 24 en suite rooms, 24-hour reception and security, and residents' bar. Green Tourism Scheme Gold Award member. Minutes' walk to main attractions and venues.
Facilities:	Rooms: General:

BRIGHTON

C Breeze Hotel ♦♦♦Guest Accommodation

12a Upper Rock Gardens, Brighton, BN2 1QE

T:	+44 (0) 1273 602608
E:	bookings@c-breezehotel.co.uk
W:	c-breezehotel.co.uk
Bedrooms:	7
Prices:	£45.00-£90.00 per double room per night, breakfast included Debit/credit card accepted
Open:	Year round
Description:	Welcoming and charming small hotel. Individually designed en suite rooms. Delicious breakfasts. Evening meals by arrangement. Children and pets welcome. Near the sea and a short walk to the Lanes, Conference venues, shopping and restaurants.
Facilities:	Rooms: General:

BRIGHTON

Funchal Guesthouse ♦♦♦Guest Accommodation

17 Madeira Place, Brighton, BN2 1TN

T:	+44 (0) 1273 603975
Bedrooms:	6
Prices:	£40.00-£60.00 per double room per night, breakfast included Debit/credit card accepted
Open:	Year round except Christmas
Description:	Our family-run guesthouse has, for more than 40 years, provided excellent breakfasts, cosy rooms, good value for money and is highly recommended.
Facilities:	Rooms: TV General:

BRIGHTON

Pavilion Guesthouse ★★★Guest Accommodation

12 Madeira Place, Brighton, BN2 1TN

T:	+44 (0) 1273 683195
E:	pavilionguesthouse@hotmail.com
W:	pavilionguesthouse.co.uk
Bedrooms:	7
Prices:	£34.00-£84.00 per double room per night, breakfast included
Open:	Year round
Description:	Just off the seafront close to all city attractions. All rooms include colour TV, radio alarm, hospitality tray, central heating and access 24 hours with own key. Open all year with a quality English or vegetarian breakfast served daily.
Facilities:	Rooms: General:

BRIGHTON

Sandpiper Guesthouse ♦♦♦Guest Accommodation

11 Russell Square, Brighton, BN1 2EE

T:	+44 (0) 1273 328202
E:	sandpiper@brighton.co.uk
Bedrooms:	8
Prices:	£30.00-£98.00 per double room per night, breakfast included Debit/credit card accepted
Open:	Year round
Description:	City centre location, close to the seafront. All rooms with central heating, colour TV, and tea-/coffee-making facilities. Front rooms with sea views. Internet access on request.
Facilities:	Rooms: General:

BRIGHTON

University of Brighton ★★/★★★Campus

Conference Office, University of Brighton, Room 228, Brighton, BN2 4AT

T:	+44 (0) 1273 6431 6764
E:	conferences@brighton.ac.uk
W:	brighton.ac.uk
Bedrooms:	111
Prices:	£16.43-£30.00 per person per night, breakfast included Debit/credit card accepted
Open:	Seasonal opening – contact for details
Description:	We have plenty of rooms at affordable prices with free car parking. Prices vary according to property and location. Weekend rate starts from £75 per person. Weekly stays also available. Please send for brochures.
Facilities:	General: P

BURGESS HILL

87 Meadow Lane ♦♦♦Guest Accommodation

87 Meadow Lane, Burgess Hill, RH15 9JD

T:	+44 (0) 1444 248421
E:	bsayers@onetel.net.uk
Bedrooms:	6
Prices:	£45.00-£50.00 per double room per night, breakfast included
Open:	Seasonal opening
Description:	Share our comfortable, detached, family home. Station, bus stop, town centre, industrial estate within easy walking distance. Car park facilities.
Facilities:	Rooms: TV General: P

HASSOCKS

New Close Farm ★★★★Guest Accommodation

London Road, Hassocks, BN6 9ND

T:	+44 (0) 1273 843144
E:	sharon.ballard@newclosefarm.co.uk
W:	newclosefarm.co.uk
Bedrooms:	2
Prices:	£45.00-£50.00 per double room per night, breakfast included
Open:	Year round
Description:	A charming 16thC granary and stable block, converted to provide self-contained accommodation with en suite facilities in a quiet location.
Facilities:	Rooms: General: P Leisure:

LANCING

Edelweiss Guesthouse ♦♦♦Guest Accommodation

Kings Road, Lancing, BN15 8EB

T:	+44 (0) 1903 753412
Bedrooms:	3
Prices:	£38.00-£42.00 per twin room per night, breakfast included
Open:	Seasonal opening – contact for details
Description:	Quietly situated just off A259. All ground-floor rooms. Family run. Non-smokers only please.
Facilities:	Rooms: General: P

LEWES

Lower Tulleys Wells Farm ★★★Guest Accommodation

Beechwood Lane/East Chiltington Road, Cooksbridge, Lewes, BN7 3QG

T:	+44 (0) 1273 472622
Bedrooms:	2
Prices:	£40.00-£50.00 per double room per night, breakfast included Cheques/cash accepted
Open:	Year round except Christmas
Description:	17thC flint farmhouse on a working farm close to South Downs and one hour by train to London. Ample parking.
Facilities:	Rooms: General: P

NEWHAVEN

Newhaven Lodge ♦♦♦Guest Accommodation

12 Brighton Road, Newhaven, BN9 9NB

T:	+44 (0) 1273 513736
Bedrooms:	7
Prices:	£45.00-£50.00 per double room per night, room only Debit/credit card, cheques/cash accepted
Open:	Year round
Description:	Comfortable and bright family-run establishment whose motto is: "Arrive as a guest and leave as a friend".
Facilities:	Rooms: General: P

STEYNING

Old Tollgate Restaurant and Hotel ★★★Hotel

The Street, Bramber, Steyning, BN44 3WE

T: **E:** **W:**	+44 (0) 1903 879494 info@oldtollgatehotel.com oldtollgatehotel.com
Bedrooms:	98
Prices:	£45.00-£112.00 per double room per night, breakfast included Debit/credit card accepted
Open:	Year round
Description:	Hotel and restaurant in historic old village at the foot of the proposed South Downs National Park.
Facilities:	General:

WORTHING

Blair House Hotel ♦♦♦♦Guest Accommodation

11 St Georges Road, Worthing, BN11 2DS

T: **E:** **W:**	+44 (0) 1903 234071 stay@blairhousehotel.co.uk blairhousehotel.co.uk
Bedrooms:	14
Prices:	£26.00-£30.00 per double room per night, room only Debit/credit card accepted
Open:	Year round
Description:	Under the personal supervision of the proprietor, close to town centre and amenities, two minutes from the sea and bowling green. Secure parking.
Facilities:	Rooms: General:

BISHOPSTON

Basca Guesthouse ★★★B&B

19 Broadway Road, Bishopston, BS7 8ES

T:	+44 (0) 117 942 2182
Bedrooms:	4
Prices:	£46.00-£48.00 per twin room per night, breakfast included
Open:	Seasonal opening – contact for details
Description:	Lovely Victorian house in quiet and leafy residential area just a short distance from the restaurants and shops of Gloucester Road. Friendly atmosphere and good food.
Facilities:	Call for details

BRISTOL

Centaur ★★★B&B

Ham Lane, Bristol, BS39 5TZ

T:	+44 (0) 1275 332321
Bedrooms:	3
Prices:	£43.00 per twin room per night, breakfast included Cheques/cash accepted
Open:	Seasonal opening – contact for details
Description:	A comfortable family house in the peaceful Chew Valley. Bishop Sutton is on the A368 between Bath and Weston-super-Mare.
Facilities:	Rooms: General: P

BRISTOL

Orchard House ★★★Guest Accommodation

Bristol Road, Chew Stoke, Bristol, BS40 8UB

T:	+44 (0) 1275 333143
E:	orchardhse@ukgateway.net
W:	orchardhse.ukgateway.net
Bedrooms:	4
Prices:	£47.00-£50.00 per double room per night, breakfast included Debit/credit card, cheques/cash accepted
Open:	Year round
Description:	Orchard House provides comfortable accommodation in a friendly, family-run 18thC house and coach house annexe. Good food using local produce. Ample parking.
Facilities:	Rooms: General: P

BRISTOL

The Paddock ♦♦♦Guest Accommodation

Hung Road, Bristol, BS11 9XJ

T:	+44 (0) 117 923 5140
Bedrooms:	6
Prices:	£25.00-£50.00 per double room per night, breakfast included
Open:	Year round except Christmas and New Year
Description:	Modern detached house set in approximately an acre of grounds with high quality accommodation.
Facilities:	Call for details

BRISTOL

The White House ♦♦♦Guest Accommodation

28 Dean Lane, Southville, Bristol, BS3 1DB

T:	+44 (0) 117 953 7725
Bedrooms:	12
Prices:	£40.00-£50.00 per twin room per night, breakfast included Debit/credit card, cheques/cash, euros accepted
Open:	Year round
Description:	Clean and comfortable guesthouse five minutes' walk from the city centre. Close to the harbour and most attractions the city of Bristol offers.
Facilities:	Rooms: General: P

BRISTOL

Treborough ♦♦♦Guest Accommodation

3 Grove Road, Coombe Dingle, Bristol, BS9 2RQ

T:	+44 (0) 117 968 2712
Bedrooms:	3
Prices:	£20.00-£40.00 per twin room per night, breakfast included
Open:	Seasonal opening – contact for details
Description:	Treborough is architecturally interesting, possessing original red hanging tiles, set in conservation area of Blaise estate. Easy access to city centre and motorways.
Facilities:	Call for details

BRISTOL

Tyndall's Park Hotel

Rating applied for

4 Tyndall's Park Road, Clifton, Bristol, BS8 1PG

T:	+44 (0) 117 973 5407
E:	contactus@tyndallsparkhotel.co.uk
W:	tyndallsparkhotel.co.uk
Bedrooms:	15
Prices:	£48.00-£58.00 per double room per night, breakfast included Debit/credit card accepted
Open:	Seasonal opening – contact for details
Description:	An elegant 15-bed hotel situated in the heart of Clifton.
Facilities:	Rooms: General: P

HARBOURSIDE

Bristol YHA

★★Hostel

14 Narrow Quay, Harbourside, BS1 4QA

T:	+44 (0) 117 922 1659
E:	bristol@yha.org.uk
W:	yha.org.uk
Bedrooms:	32
Prices:	£14.50-£25.00 per person per night, breakfast included
Open:	Year round
Description:	Impressive refurbished warehouse on the quayside in Bristol's historic harbour area set in the heart of the city.
Facilities:	Call for details

CAMBRIDGE

Manor Farm

♦♦♦♦Guest Accommodation

Green End, Landbeach, Cambridge, CB4 8ED

T:	+44 (0) 1223 860165
Bedrooms:	3
Prices:	£45.00-£50.00 per double room per night, breakfast included
Open:	Year round
Description:	Grade II Listed, double-fronted, Georgian farmhouse, surrounded by enclosed garden. In centre of village next to church.
Facilities:	Rooms: General: P

BRISTOL

CAMBRIDGE

CAMBRIDGE

Southampton Guesthouse ★★★Guest Accommodation

7 Elizabeth Way, Cambridge, CB4 1DE

T:	+44 (0) 1223 357780
E:	southamptonhouse@telco4u.net
W:	southamptonguesthouse.com
Bedrooms:	4
Prices:	£48.00 per twin room per night, room only
Open:	Year round
Description:	Well situated close to the shopping centre, most comfortable and with a car parking space.
Facilities:	Rooms: General: **P**

CHERRY HINTON

Old Rosemary Branch ★★B&B

The Old Rosemary Branch, Cherry Hinton, CB1 3LF

T:	+44 (0) 1223 247161
E:	s.anderson@constructionplus.net
W:	theoldrosemarybranch.co.uk
Bedrooms:	3
Prices:	£45.00 per twin room per night, room only
Open:	Year round
Description:	Friendly, comfortable, family house dating to mid-1700s.
Facilities:	Rooms: General:

STAPLEFORD

Riverside Stables ♦♦♦♦Guest Accommodation

8 Bury Road, Stapleford, CB2 5BP

T:	+44 (0) 1223 565863
E:	pamagarland@hotmail.com
W:	riversidestables.co.uk
Bedrooms:	2
Prices:	£35.00 per twin room per night, room only
Open:	Year round
Description:	Beautiful, modern home with stabling in rural setting close to Cambridge. Bus/train, village shop and pubs serving food are close by.
Facilities:	Leisure: U

TOFT

Meadowview

★★★★B&B

3 Brookside, Toft, Cambridgeshire, CB3 7RJ

T: +44 (0) 1223 263395
E: carol@meadowview.co.uk
W: meadowview.co.uk

Bedrooms: 2

Prices: £48.00 per twin room per night, room only

Open: Year round

Description: Meadowview is a large, family house situated on the edge of a small rural village, overlooking fields where a warm welcome awaits our guests.

Facilities: Rooms:
General: P
Leisure:

CARLISLE

Ashleigh House

★★★★Guesthouse

46 Victoria Place, Carlisle, CA1 1EX

T: +44 (0) 1228 521631

Bedrooms: 7

Prices: £45.00-£50.00 per double room per night, breakfast included
Debit/credit card, cheques/cash accepted

Open: Year round except Christmas and New Year

Description: Well-appointed guesthouse close to city amenities, bus and rail stations. Convenient for The Lakes, Scottish Borders, Hadrian's Wall and Settle Line.

Facilities: Rooms: TV
General:

CARLISLE

Avar House

♦♦♦♦Guest Accommodation

12 Scotland Road, Carlisle, CA3 9DG

SILVER AWARD

T: +44 (0) 1228 540636
E: guesthouse@avarhouse.fslife.co.uk
W: avarhouse.co.uk

Bedrooms: 5

Prices: £45.00 per double room per night, breakfast included

Open: Year round

Description: Family-run environment, a relaxed home-from-home feel. Will do our utmost to make your stay enjoyable.

Facilities: Rooms:
General:

CARLISLE

Brooklyn House ♦♦♦Guest Accommodation

42 Victoria Place, Carlisle, CA1 1EX

T:	+44 (0) 1228 590002
Bedrooms:	3
Prices:	£18.00-£20.00 per single room per night, breakfast included Euros accepted
Open:	Year round
Description:	Family-run Grade II Listed Victorian townhouse, two minutes' walk from city centre. All children welcome.
Facilities:	Rooms: General:

CARLISLE

Cartref Guesthouse ★★★★Guesthouse

44 Victoria Place, Carlisle, CA1 1EX SILVER AWARD

T:	+44 (0) 1228 522077
Bedrooms:	8
Prices:	£40.00-£45.00 per double room per night, breakfast included Cheques/cash accepted
Open:	Year round
Description:	Cartref, recently refurbished and under new management boasts a home-from-home atmosphere. Offers full English breakfast plus evening meals.
Facilities:	Rooms: TV General: P

CARLISLE

Courtfield House ★★★★Guesthouse

169 Warwick Road, Carlisle, CA1 1LP SILVER AWARD

T:	+44 (0) 1228 522767
Bedrooms:	8
Prices:	£44.00-£50.00 per double room per night, breakfast included
Open:	Seasonal opening – contact for details
Description:	Large Victorian townhouse with en suite facilities close to the city centre and all amenities. Easy access for rail, coach stations and the M6.
Facilities:	Call for details

CARLISLE

Fernlee Guesthouse ♦♦♦♦Guest Accommodation

9 St Aidans Road, Carlisle, CA1 1LT

T:	+44 (0) 1228 511930
Bedrooms:	Call for details
Prices:	£25.00-£30.00 per single room per night, breakfast included
Open:	Year round
Description:	Family-run guesthouse, warm welcome awaits everyone, no age limit for children. After a good night's sleep in our very comfortable, well-decorated bedrooms, a good hearty breakfast awaits you. Vegetarians also catered for. Arrivals anytime.
Facilities:	Rooms: General: P Leisure:

CARLISLE

Hazeldean Guesthouse ★★★Guesthouse

Orton Grange, Wigton Road, Carlisle, CA5 6LA

T: **E:** **W:**	+44 (0) 1228 711953 hazeldean1@btopenworld.com smoothhound.co.uk/hotels/hazeldean.html
Bedrooms:	4
Prices:	£40.00-£44.00 per double room per night, breakfast included
Open:	Year round
Description:	Detached property with safe parking and large garden with picnic area. Warm, friendly atmosphere with large lounge and dining area. Close to local bus route for Carlisle and Lake District.
Facilities:	Rooms: General: P

CARLISLE

Hillside Farm ★★★B&B

Boustead Hill, Burgh-by-Sands, Carlisle, CA5 6AA

T: **E:** **W:**	+44 (0) 1228 576398 ruddshillside1@btinternet.com hadrianswalkbnb.co.uk
Bedrooms:	2
Prices:	£40.00 per double room per night, breakfast included
Open:	Year round
Description:	Come and stay in a Georgian Grade II Listed farmhouse built in 1856 on the Solway Coast. With outstanding views towards Scotland over the Solway marshes. We are steps away from Hadrian's Wall on the Coast to Coast cycle route.
Facilities:	Rooms: General:

CARLISLE

Howard Lodge ♦♦♦♦Guest Accommodation

90 Warwick Road, Carlisle, CA1 1JU

T: +44 (0) 1228 529842
E: chrltdavi@aol.com
W: howard-lodge.co.uk

Bedrooms: 7

Prices: £40.00-£50.00 per double room per night, breakfast included
Euros accepted

Open: Year round

Description: All rooms en suite. Private car parking. Close to bus and railway station. One mile from junction 43 on M6 motorway. Five minutes' walk to town centre and all its amenities.

Facilities: Rooms:
General: P
Leisure:

CARLISLE

Rosemount Cottage ♦♦♦♦Guest Accommodation

Rosemount, Burgh-by-Sands, Carlisle, CA5 6AN

T: +44 (0) 1228 576440
E: tweentown@aol.com
W: rosemountcottage.co.uk

Bedrooms: 3

Prices: £40.00-£50.00 per double room per night, breakfast included
Euros accepted

Open: Year round

Description: Grade II Listed cottage in Solway village of Burgh-by-Sands on Hadrian's Wall trail. Three guest rooms, two guest bathrooms, sitting room and kitchen. Pub 250 yards for meals, Carlisle five miles. Cottage also available for self-catering rental.

Facilities: Rooms:
General: P

CARLISLE

The Steadings ♦♦♦Guest Accommodation

Townhead Farm, Houghton, Carlisle, CA6 4JB

T: +44 (0) 1228 523019
W: thesteadings.co.uk

Bedrooms: 2

Prices: £40.00-£50.00 per double room per night, breakfast included

Open: Year round

Description: Kitchen for residents' use. Self-contained barn conversions, own front door, key for easy access anytime. Very near Roman Wall route.

Facilities: Rooms:
General: P

CARLISLE

Townhouse B&B ★★★★Guest Accommodation

153 Warwick Road, Carlisle, CA1 1LU

T:	+44 (0) 1228 598782
E:	townhouse@christine60.freeserve.co.uk
W:	townhouse-bandb.com
Bedrooms:	5
Prices:	£45.00-£50.00 per double room per night, breakfast included
Open:	Year round
Description:	Minutes' walk away – city centre, castle, museum and cathedral five; municipal golf course two; Sands centre, leisure centre and entertainment centre five. By car to the Lake District 40 minutes; Scottish Borders 20 minutes.
Facilities:	Rooms: General: Leisure:

CARLISLE

Vallum Barn ★★★★B&B

Irthington, Carlisle, CA6 4NN SILVER AWARD

T:	+44 (0) 1697 742478
E:	vallumbarn@tinyworld.co.uk
W:	vallumbarn.co.uk
Bedrooms:	2
Prices:	£23.00-£50.00 per person per night, breakfast included
Open:	Year round
Description:	Spacious, converted barn easily accessible from M6 and only five minutes' walk from the country pub. Ground floor room suitable for disabled guests. Two family bedrooms, children and very well behaved dogs welcome.
Facilities:	Rooms: General: P

CARLISLE

Wallfoot Hotel and Restaurant ★★Hotel

Park Broom, Crosby-on-Eden, Carlisle, CA6 4QH

T:	+44 (0) 1228 573696
Bedrooms:	6
Prices:	£44.00-£50.00 per double room per night, breakfast included Debit/credit card, cheques/cash accepted
Open:	Year round except Christmas and New Year
Description:	Enjoy a warm welcome and good food at this friendly, family-owned hotel. Located in beautiful countryside en route for Hadrian's Wall, yet only three minutes from the M6.
Facilities:	Rooms: General: P Leisure:

CARLISLE

White Lea Guesthouse ★★★★B&B

191 Warwick Road, Carlisle, CA1 1LP

T:	+44 (0) 1228 533139
Bedrooms:	4
Prices:	£40.00-£45.00 per double room per night, breakfast included
Open:	Year round
Description:	Friendly, family-run, guesthouse, clean rooms, comfortable beds, great breakfasts and great conversations.
Facilities:	Rooms: General: **P**

CHESTER

Carmeletta ♦♦♦Guest Accommodation

16-18 Hough Green, Chester, CH4 8JG

T: **E:** **W:**	+44 (0) 1244 677876 info@carmeletta.co.uk carmeletta.co.uk
Bedrooms:	6
Prices:	£45.00 per double room per night, breakfast included
Open:	Seasonal opening – contact for details
Description:	Family-run establishment, charming hostess, home from home atmosphere. Private car park to rear.
Facilities:	Rooms: TV General: **P**

CHESTER

Chester Brooklands ★★★Guest Accommodation

8 Newton Lane, Hoole, Chester, CH2 3RB

T:	+44 (0) 1244 348856
Bedrooms:	4
Prices:	£34.00-£80.00 per double room per night, breakfast included
Open:	Seasonal opening – contact for details
Description:	A Victorian property offering four, large, well-equipped bedrooms, each with good sized en suites. A pleasant welcome awaits all.
Facilities:	Call for details

CHESTER

Chippings

★★★★Guest Accommodation

10 Cranford Court, Chester, CH4 7LN

T: +44 (0) 1244 679728
E: chippings@keme.co.uk
W: visitchester.com

Bedrooms: 2

Prices: £45.00-£60.00 per double room per night, breakfast included

Open: Seasonal opening – contact for details

Description: Owners are waiting to welcome you to a newly furnished en suite room. Eat your breakfast on the patio (weather permitting) and watch the birds queue up to take their early morning bath!

Facilities: Rooms:
General: P

CHESTER

Dene Hotel

★★Hotel

Hoole Road, Hoole, Chester, CH2 3ND

T: +44 (0) 1244 321165
E: info@denehotel.com
W: denehotel.com

Bedrooms: 11

Prices: £45.00-£79.00 per double room per night, breakfast included
Debit/credit card accepted

Open: Year round

Description: Only five minutes from Chester Zoo and the city centre. Special deals available. Near to motorway and rail station.

Facilities: Rooms:
General: P

CHESTER

Eastern Guesthouse

★★B&B

Eastern Pathway, Chester, CH4 7AQ

T: +44 (0) 1244 680104

Bedrooms: 3

Prices: £40.00 per double room per night, breakfast included

Open: Seasonal opening – contact for details

Description: Small, family-run guesthouse in a quiet area just 10 minutes' walk from the city centre. All rooms en suite. Late arrivals by arrangement. Special three-night breaks.

Facilities: Rooms:
General: P

CHESTER

Ford Farm ♦♦♦Guest Accommodation

Newton Lane, Tattenhall, Chester, CH3 9NE

T:	+44 (0) 1829 770307
Bedrooms:	3
Prices:	£40.00 per double room per night, breakfast included
Open:	Seasonal opening – contact for details
Description:	A friendly welcome to a working farm in beautiful countryside with views of Beeston and Peckforton Castles. Six miles south of Chester. Ideal base to visit Chester and the Welsh countryside.
Facilities:	Rooms: General: P Leisure:

CHESTER

Garden Gate Guesthouse ★★★Guesthouse

8 Chester Street, Nr Saltney, Chester, CH4 8BJ

T: **E:**	+44 (0) 1244 682306 dollywal@msn.com
Bedrooms:	10
Prices:	£40.00-£45.00 per double room per night, breakfast included
Open:	Seasonal opening – contact for details
Description:	On good bus route for city centre, 10 rooms, good clean accommodation. Close to golf course and park. Last arrival 21:45. Comfortable and friendly.
Facilities:	Rooms: General: P Leisure:

CHESTER

Hameldaeus ★★★B&B

9 Lorne Street, Chester, CH1 4AE

T: **E:**	+44 (0) 1244 374913 joyce_brunton@tiscali.co.uk
Bedrooms:	3
Prices:	£48.00 per double room per night, breakfast included
Open:	Seasonal opening – contact for details
Description:	Comfortable B&B with a private garden and patio area, close to city centre attractions, canal and river and leisure centre.
Facilities:	Rooms: General:

CHESTER

Holly House ★★★B&B

41 Liverpool Road, Chester, CH2 1AB

T: +44 (0) 1244 383484
E: fjb5@tutor.open.ac.uk

Bedrooms: 3

Prices: £44.00 per double room per night, breakfast included

Open: Seasonal opening – contact for details

Description: An elegant Victorian house with the emphasis on comfort and friendliness, rooms are spacious and well equipped. Town centre shops, restaurants and other attractions all within easy walking distance. Off-road parking available.

Facilities: Rooms:
General: P

CHESTER

Kings Guesthouse ♦♦♦♦Guest Accommodation

14 Eaton Road, Handbridge, Chester, CH4 7EN

T: +44 (0) 1244 671249
E: king@kings.plus.com

Bedrooms: 7

Prices: £44.00 per double room per night, breakfast included
Debit/credit card accepted

Open: Seasonal opening – contact for details

Description: Newly refurbished and just a short walk from city centre. Large car park, all rooms en suite with hairdryers, tea-/coffee-making facilities.

Facilities: Rooms:
General: P

CHESTER

Laurels ★★★★B&B

14 Selkirk Road, Curzon Park, Chester, CH4 8AH

T: +44 (0) 1244 679682
E: howell@ellisroberts.freeserve.co.uk

Bedrooms: 3

Prices: £25.00-£26.00 per double room per night, breakfast included

Open: Seasonal opening – contact for details

Description: Quiet, residential area near racecourse and river. Within easy walking distance to the city centre. Parking on drive. Key to front door.

Facilities: Rooms:
General: P

CHESTER

Lavender Lodge

Rating applied for

Hoole Road, Chester, CH2 3NL

T:	+44 (0) 1244 323204
Bedrooms:	5
Prices:	£40.00-£70.00 per double room per night, breakfast included Debit/credit card accepted
Open:	Year round
Description:	Conveniently located in Hoole Village in close proximity to shops and restaurants. Flexible arrival and departure times (within reason).
Facilities:	Rooms: General: P

CHESTER

Tentry Heys

★★★B&B

Queens Park Road, Chester, CH4 7AD

T:	+44 (0) 1244 677857
Bedrooms:	3
Prices:	£44.00 per double room per night, breakfast included
Open:	Seasonal opening – contact for details
Description:	A warm welcome is extended to this Victorian guesthouse in own grounds. Picturesque, six minutes' walk to city centre. Private parking. En suite and all rooms colour TV, tea-/coffee-making facilities, central heating. Discount breaks on request.
Facilities:	Rooms: General: P

TARPORLEY

Foresters Arms

★★★Inn

92 High Street, Tarporley, CW6 0AX

T: **E:**	+44 (0) 1829 733151 stuart@forestersarms.fsbusiness.co.uk
Bedrooms:	2
Prices:	£45.00-£60.00 per double room per night, breakfast included Debit/credit card accepted
Open:	Seasonal opening – contact for details
Description:	A country public house on the edge of Tarporley. Offering a homely and friendly service. Weekly rates negotiable.
Facilities:	Rooms: General: P Leisure:

BOGNOR REGIS

Sea Crest Private Hotel ♦♦♦Guest Accommodation

Nyewood Lane, Bognor Regis, PO21 2QB

T:	+44 (0) 1243 821438
Bedrooms:	6
Prices:	£40.00-£50.00 per double room per night, breakfast included
Open:	Year round except Christmas and New Year
Description:	Small, private hotel near the sea with modern en suite rooms.
Facilities:	Rooms: [icons] General: P [icons]

CHICHESTER

5a Little London ♦♦♦Guest Accommodation

Little London, Chichester, PO19 1PH

T:	+44 (0) 1243 788405
Bedrooms:	1
Prices:	£27.50-£50.00 per single room per night, breakfast included
Open:	Year round
Description:	Town house in city centre. Stairs to first floor, single bedroom. Continental breakfast available.
Facilities:	Rooms: [icons] General: [icons]

CHICHESTER

Apiary Cottage ♦♦♦Guest Accommodation

Compton, Chichester, PO18 9EX

T:	+44 (0) 23 9263 1306
Bedrooms:	5
Prices:	£25.00-£40.00 per double room per night, breakfast included
Open:	Year round
Description:	Pretty, Victorian cottage nestling at the foot of the Downs. Peaceful surrounding and beautiful views. Ideal for walking and cycling, Goodwood and Chichester. Large car park. Children welcome.
Facilities:	General: P [icons]

CHICHESTER

Brufords
♦♦♦♦Guest Accommodation

66/66A The Street, Boxgrove, Chichester, PO18 0EE

T: +44 (0) 1243 774085
E: room4me@brufords.org
W: brufords.org

Bedrooms: 5

Prices: £40.00-£70.00 per double room per night, breakfast included
Debit/credit card accepted

Open: Year round

Description: Only five minutes from Chichester and Goodwood. All rooms en suite and all rooms have a fridge. Some have a microwave.

Facilities: Rooms:
General:

CHICHESTER

Eastmere House
★★★B&B

Eastergate Lane, Eastergate, Chichester, PO20 3SJ

T: +44 (0) 1243 544204
E: bernardlane@hotmail.com
W: eastmere.com

Bedrooms: 3

Prices: £40.00-£70.00 per double room per night, breakfast included
Euros accepted

Open: Seasonal opening – contact for details

Description: Eastmere House is between Arundel and Chichester. Two double-rooms and one twin room with TV, spacious bathroom, large shower, cottage gardens, guest lounge and hearty breakfast.

Facilities: Rooms:
General: P
Leisure:

CHICHESTER

Kia-ora
♦♦♦Guest Accommodation

Main Road, Nutbourne, Chichester, PO18 8RT

T: +44 (0) 1243 572858
E: KiaoraBandB@aol.com

Bedrooms: 1

Prices: £45.00-£50.00 per double room per night, breakfast included
Euros accepted

Open: Seasonal opening – closed New Year

Description: Open views to Chichester harbour. Warm welcome in comfortable family house. Large garden. Restaurants and country pubs within walking distance.

Facilities: General:

CHICHESTER

Litten House
♦♦♦Guest Accommodation

148 St Pancras, Chichester, PO19 7SH

T:	+44 (0) 1243 774503
E:	victoria@littenho.demon.co.uk
W:	littenho.demon.co.uk
Bedrooms:	3
Prices:	£48.00 per double room per night, breakfast included Debit/credit card, euros accepted
Open:	Year round
Description:	Georgian house in city centre, near theatre, station, shops, restaurants. King size bed. Double room with private balcony.
Facilities:	General: ❊

CHICHESTER

Lodge Hill Farm
★★★Farmhouse

West Dean, Chichester, PO18 0RT

T:	+44 (0) 1243 535245
Bedrooms:	3
Prices:	£44.00-£50.00 per double room per night, breakfast included
Open:	Seasonal opening – contact for details
Description:	Flint farmhouse built in 1813 on the South Downs, superb views, near Goodwood, 15 minutes to Chichester, ideal for walkers.
Facilities:	Rooms: [symbols] General: P [symbols]

CHICHESTER

Longmeadow
♦♦♦Guest Accommodation

Pine Grove, Chichester, PO19 3PN

T:	+44 (0) 1243 782063
E:	bbeeching@lineone.net
W:	longmeadowguesthouse.com
Bedrooms:	3
Prices:	£27.00-£35.00 per twin room per night, breakfast included
Open:	Year round
Description:	Annexe accommodation overlooking garden in country setting. Near to theatre and Goodwood racecourse.
Facilities:	General: ❊

CHICHESTER

The Cornerways ♦♦♦♦Guest Accommodation

73 Hillfield Road, Selsey, Chichester, PO20 0LF

T:	+44 (0) 1243 605859
Bedrooms:	3
Prices:	£25.00-£30.00 per double room per night, breakfast included Cheques/cash, euros accepted
Open:	Year round except Christmas and New Year
Description:	Detached, 100-year-old house in quiet location, 200 yards from the sea.
Facilities:	Rooms: General: P

HAYLING ISLAND

Ann's Cottage ★★B&B

45 St Andrews Road, Hayling Island, PO11 9JN

T: **E:**	+44 (0) 23 9246 7048 ann.jay@virgin.net
Bedrooms:	3
Prices:	£49.98 per double room per night, breakfast included
Open:	Year round
Description:	Pretty, detached bungalow overlooking parkland 50 yards from the beach. Good English breakfast and comfortable accommodation. Garden and car parking available. Convenient, quiet and within easy reach of Portsmouth, Goodwood and Chichester.
Facilities:	Rooms: General: P

HAYLING ISLAND

Seaventure ♦♦♦♦Guest Accommodation

20 Manor Way, Hayling Island, PO11 9JH

T: **E:** **W:**	+44 (0) 23 9234 6093 patanddavids@tesco.net seaventure.co.uk
Bedrooms:	3
Prices:	£49.50-£55.00 per double room per night, breakfast included
Open:	Year round except Christmas and New Year
Description:	Small guesthouse 200 yards from beach. Tea-/coffee-making facilities, TV, video, fridge. Overnight storage sailboards etc. Drying, wash down, freezer facilities.
Facilities:	Rooms: General: P Leisure:

HAYLING ISLAND

The Coach House
★★★★Guest Accommodation

Church Lane, Hayling Island, PO11 0SB
SILVER AWARD

T: +44 (0) 23 9246 6266
E: jenny.stenning1@btinternet.com
W: up.to/coachhouse

Bedrooms: 1

Prices: £25.00-£35.00 per person per night, breakfast included

Open: Year round except Christmas and New Year

Description: The Coach House stands within the quiet grounds of a 17thC farmhouse; having spacious (40ft) accommodation with en suite facilities.

Facilities: Rooms:
General: P

COVENTRY

Acacia Guesthouse
★★★★Guesthouse

11 Park Road, Coventry, CV1 2LE

T: +44 (0) 24 7663 3622
E: acaciaguesthouse@hotmail.com

Bedrooms: 14

Prices: £30.00-£49.50 per double room per night, breakfast included

Open: Year round

Description: Hotel quality with guesthouse charm. Just a short walk from the railway station, city centre, and bus station.

Facilities: Rooms:
General: P

COVENTRY

Ashleigh House
★★★Guesthouse

17 Park Road, Coventry, CV1 2LE

T: +44 (0) 24 7622 3804

Bedrooms: 10

Prices: £35.00-£63.00 per double room per night, breakfast included

Open: Year round

Description: Experience a warm welcome from friendly, helpful staff. Well maintained and equipped en suite accommodation. All city amenities and railway station within a five minute walk.

Facilities: Rooms:
General: P

COVENTRY

Barnacle Farm

★★★★Farmhouse

Back Lane, Meriden, Coventry, CV7 7LD

T:	+44 (0) 24 7646 8875
Bedrooms:	3
Prices:	£27.50-£48.00 per twin room per night, breakfast included
Open:	Year round
Description:	Property set in a truly rural position. Convenient for the National Exhibition Centre, Birmingham International and Birmingham Airport, as well as Kenilworth, Warwick and Stratford on Avon. Eight minutes from M6 and M42.
Facilities:	Rooms: General: P Leisure:

COVENTRY

Barnacle Hall

★★★★★Farmhouse
GOLD AWARD

Shilton Lane, Shilton, Coventry, CV7 9LH

T:	+44 (0) 24 7661 2629
E:	rose@barnaclehall.co.uk
W:	barnaclehall.co.uk
Bedrooms:	3
Prices:	£30.00-£60.00 per double room per night, breakfast included
Open:	Year round
Description:	A 16thC farmhouse offering high quality B&B in a rural location with easy motorway access.
Facilities:	Rooms: General: P Leisure:

COVENTRY

Bede Guesthouse

★★★B&B

250 Radford Road, Radford, Coventry, CV6 3BV

T:	+44 (0) 24 7659 7837
E:	bedehouse@aol.com
Bedrooms:	3
Prices:	£25.00-£30.00 per person per night, breakfast included Debit/credit card accepted
Open:	Year round
Description:	We are based near the city centre. All rooms have ensuite and TVs, tea-/coffee-making facilities. Rooms changed daily and the guests have added peace of mind of secure parking.
Facilities:	Rooms: General: P

COVENTRY

Bonnifinglas Guesthouse ★★★Guesthouse

3 Berkswell Road, Meriden, Coventry, CV7 7LB

T:	+44 (0) 1676 523193
W:	bonnifinglas.co.uk
Bedrooms:	8
Prices:	£45.00 per double room per night, breakfast included Cheques/cash, euros accepted
Open:	Year round except Christmas and New Year
Description:	Country house, all rooms en suite with TV. Several pubs and restaurants in walking distance.
Facilities:	Rooms: General: P Leisure:

COVENTRY

Camp Farm ★★★Guest Accommodation

Hob Lane, Coventry, CV7 7GX

T:	+44 (0) 1676 533804
Bedrooms:	3
Prices:	£45.00-£47.00 per double room per night, breakfast included
Open:	Year round
Description:	This 200-year-old farmhouse was used as a campsite by Cromwell for the seige of Kenilworth. Friendly home-from-home.
Facilities:	Rooms: General: P

COVENTRY

Highcroft Guesthouse ★★★Guest Accommodation

65 Barras Lane, Coundon, Coventry, CV1 4AQ

T:	+44 (0) 24 7622 8157
E:	deepakcov@hotmail.com
Bedrooms:	7
Prices:	£25.00-£53.00 per double room per night, breakfast included
Open:	Year round
Description:	Family-run business with individual charm and style, offering high standard accommodation and excellent value. Close to city centre. Secure on-site parking.
Facilities:	Rooms: General: P

COVENTRY

Merlyn Guesthouse ★★★Guesthouse

105 Holyhead Road, Coventry, CV1 3AD

T:	+44 (0) 24 7622 2800
Bedrooms:	12
Prices:	£45.00-£60.00 per double room per night, breakfast included Debit/credit card, cheques/cash, euros accepted
Open:	Year round
Description:	Modern guesthouse, close to the city centre, family-run. Many facilities with value for money approach.
Facilities:	Rooms: General: P Leisure:

COVENTRY

Spire View Guesthouse ★★★Guest Accommodation

36 Park Road, Coventry, CV1 2LD

T:	+44 (0) 24 7625 1602
E:	bookings@spireviewguesthouse.co.uk
W:	spireviewguesthouse.co.uk
Bedrooms:	12
Prices:	£33.00-£66.00 per double room per night, breakfast included Euros accepted
Open:	Year round
Description:	Quality run accommodation, conveniently situated a few minutes' walk from railway station, historic centre and cathedral – ideal for visiting local Warwickshire attractions. Easy access to NEC and Coventry/Birmingham airports.
Facilities:	Rooms: General: P

KENILWORTH

Best Western Peacock Hotel ★★★Hotel

149 Warwick Road, Kenilworth, CV8 1HY

T:	+44 (0) 1926 851156
E:	reservations@peacockhotel.com
W:	peacockhotel.com
Bedrooms:	29
Prices:	£49.00-£120.00 per double room per night, breakfast included Debit/credit card, cheques/cash accepted
Open:	Year round
Description:	Award-winning hotel providing outstanding quality with first class service at reasonable prices. Luxurious accomodation, a choice of three restaurants ranked "Best in Midlands", cocktail bar, and car parking. Ideally situated for short breaks.
Facilities:	Rooms: General: P Leisure:

KENILWORTH

Grounds Farm B&B ♦♦♦♦Guest Accommodation

Grounds Farm Lane, Kenilworth, CV8 1PP

T: +44 (0) 1926 864542
E: zoe@groundsfarm.com
W: groundsfarm.co.uk

Bedrooms: 4

Prices: £45.00-£60.00 per double room per night, breakfast included

Open: Seasonal opening – contact for details

Description: B&B in a traditional farmhouse, in a peaceful location enjoying magnificent views of Kenilworth Castle.

Facilities: Call for details

LEAMINGTON SPA

4 Lillington Road ★★B&B

Lillington Road, Leamington Spa, CV32 5YR

T: +44 (0) 1926 429244
E: squireburton@aol.com

Bedrooms: 3

Prices: £20.00 per double room per night, breakfast included

Open: Year round – closed New Year

Description: An attractive Victorian house situated within five minutes' walk of the town centre. Within easy reach of the NAC, NEC and Stratford-upon-Avon, Warwick and the Cotswolds.

Facilities: Rooms:
General:

LEAMINGTON SPA

Adelaide ♦♦♦Guest Accommodation

15 Adelaide Road, Leamington Spa, CV31 3PN

T: +44 (0) 1926 450633

Bedrooms: 2

Prices: £35.00-£45.00 per double room per night, room only

Open: Year round

Description: A charming, Victorian townhouse with original features, in beautiful town centre conservation area. All rooms en suite with colour TV, trouser press and tea-/coffee-making facilities. Close to the NEC and NAC.

Facilities: Rooms: TV
General: P

LEAMINGTON SPA

Avenue Lodge Guesthouse ★★★Guesthouse

61 Avenue Road, Leamington Spa, CV31 3PF

T: +44 (0) 1926 338555
E: avenue-lodge@yahoo.co.uk
W: avenue-lodge.co.uk

Bedrooms: 5

Prices: £40.00-£50.00 per double room per night, breakfast included
Cheques/cash accepted

Open: Year round – closed New Year

Description: B&B in an agreeable Victorian house with personal service. Close to town centre, railway station and motorway links.

Facilities: Rooms:
General: P

LEAMINGTON SPA

Buckland Lodge Hotel ★★★Guesthouse

35 Avenue Road, Leamington Spa, CV31 3PG

T: +44 (0) 1926 423843
E: buckland.lodge1@btinternet.com
W: Buckland-Lodge.co.uk.

Bedrooms: 10

Prices: £46.00-£48.00 per double room per night, breakfast included
Debit/credit card, cheques/cash accepted

Open: Year round except Christmas and New Year

Description: Central for rail and bus depots and shops, parks and town's beautiful gardens.

Facilities: Rooms:
General: P

LEAMINGTON SPA

Hedley Villa Guesthouse ★★★Guesthouse

31 Russell Terrace, Leamington Spa, CV31 1EZ

T: +44 (0) 1926 424504
E: hedley-villa@hotmail.com
W: eyvillaguesthouse.co.uk

Bedrooms: 9

Prices: £45.00-£50.00 per double room per night, breakfast included
Debit/credit card accepted

Open: Year round

Description: Homely guesthouse close to town centre. Convenient for National Exhibition Centre, National Agricultural Centre, Stratford, Coventry, Kenilworth, M40 and Warwick.

Facilities: Rooms:
General:

LEAMINGTON SPA

Hill Farm
♦♦♦♦Guest Accommodation

Lewis Road, Radford Semele, Royal Leamington Spa, CV31 1UX

T: +44 (0) 1926 337571
E: rebecca@hillfarm3000.fsnet.co.uk
W: hillfarm.info

Bedrooms: 16

Prices: £25.00 per double room per night, room only

Open: Year round

Description: Hill Farm is a comfortable mid-Victorian farmhouse within 350 acres of working farmland. A pleasant lounge for our visitors, leisure and light conservatory/breakfast room add to the appeal. The bedrooms are all pleasantly appointed.

Facilities: Rooms:
General: **P**

LEAMINGTON SPA

The Coach House
♦♦♦♦Guest Accommodation

Snowford Hall Farm, Hunningham, Royal Leamington Spa, CV33 9ES SILVER AWARD

T: +44 (0) 1926 632297
E: the_coach_house@lineone.net
W: ite.lineone.net/~the_coach_house

Bedrooms: 12

Prices: £22.00-£24.00 per double room per night, room only

Open: Year round

Description: A warm and friendly welcome awaits you at The Coach House. Our comfortable home is a converted barn on a 200-acre working farm and its elevated position offers wonderful views over quiet, rolling countryside. Situated just off the Fosse Way.

Facilities: Rooms:
General: **P**

LEAMINGTON SPA

Trendway Guesthouse
★★★Guesthouse

45 Avenue Road, Leamington Spa, CV31 3PF

T: +44 (0) 1926 316644
E: avenue-lodge@yahoo.co.uk
W: avenue-lodge.co.uk

Bedrooms: 5

Prices: £45.00-£50.00 per twin room per night, breakfast included

Open: Year round except Christmas and New Year

Description: A three-storey Victorian house with five letting bedrooms, just off the town centre and five minutes from railway station.

Facilities: Rooms:
General: **P**

LEAMINGTON SPA

Victoria Park Hotel ★★★★Guest Accommodation

12 Adelaide Road, Leamington Spa, CV31 3PW

T: +44 (0) 1926 424195
E: info@victoriaparkhotelleamingtonspa.co.uk
W: victoriaparkhotelleamingtonspa.co.uk

Bedrooms: 20

Prices: £45.00-£70.00 per double room per night, breakfast included
Debit/credit card, cheques/cash accepted

Open: Seasonal opening – contact for details

Description: Victorian house close to bus and railway stations and town centre. Park, pump room, gardens, bowls, tennis and river, all three minutes' walk away.

Facilities: Rooms:
General: P

LEAMINGTON SPA

Hill House ♦♦♦♦Guest Accommodation

Off Mancetter Road, Nuneaton, CV10 0RS

T: +44 (0) 24 7639 6985

Bedrooms: 3

Prices: £28.00-£48.00 per twin room per night, breakfast included

Open: Year round

Description: Comfortable home, 18 acres of park-like gardens. Panoramic views of Anker Valley Nature Centre. Traffic-free walks. Historical association. Two miles A5.

Facilities: Rooms:
General: P
Leisure:

RUGBY

White Lion Inn ♦♦♦Guest Accommodation

Coventry Road, Pailton, Rugby, CV23 0QD

T: +44 (0) 1788 832359
W: whitelionpailton.co.uk

Bedrooms: 20

Prices: £46.00-£56.00 per twin room per night, breakfast included
Debit/credit card accepted

Open: Year round

Description: Former 17thC coaching inn, recently refurbished but maintaining all old world features. Close to Rugby, Coventry and Stratford. Within four miles of all motorways.

Facilities: Rooms:
General: P
Leisure:

WARWICK

Agincourt Lodge

★★★★Guesthouse

36 Coten End, Warwick, CV34 4NP

T: +44 (0) 1926 499399
E: enquires@agincourtlodge.co.uk
W: agincourtlodge.co.uk

Bedrooms: 6

Prices: £40.00-£75.00 per double room per night, breakfast included
Debit/credit card, cheques/cash, euros accepted

Open: Year round except Christmas and New Year

Description: A Victorian family-run hotel, just five minutes from Warwick Castle, Warwick train station, and easy proximity to Royal Leamington Spa and Stratford-upon-Avon. We offer comfortable en suite rooms, some with king-size four-posters.

Facilities: Rooms:
General: P

WARWICK

Austin House

★★★Guesthouse

96 Emscote Road, Warwick, CV34 5QJ

T: +44 (0) 1926 493583
E: mike.austinhouse96@ntlworld.com
W: austinhousewarwick.co.uk

Bedrooms: 7

Prices: £42.00-£50.00 per double room per night, breakfast included
Debit/credit card, cheques/cash accepted

Open: Year round except Christmas and New Year

Description: Black-and-white Victorian house a mile from Warwick Castle, Royal Leamington Spa and eight miles from Stratford-upon-Avon.

Facilities: Rooms: TV
General: P

WARWICK

Avon Guesthouse

★★★★Guesthouse

7 Emscote Road, Warwick, CV34 4PH

T: +44 (0) 1926 491367
E: info@avonguesthouse.co.uk
W: avonguesthouse.co.uk

Bedrooms: 7

Prices: £48.00 per double room per night, breakfast included
Cheques/cash accepted

Open: Year round except Christmas and New Year

Description: A family-run guesthouse with a friendly atmosphere, in pleasant surroundings near Warwick Castle and town centre.

Facilities: Rooms: TV
General: P
Leisure:

WARWICK

Chesterfields Guesthouse

★★★Guesthouse

84 Emscote Road, Warwick, CV34 5QJ

T: +44 (0) 1926 774864
E: jchapman@chesterfields.freeserve.co.uk
W: smoothound.co.uk

Bedrooms: 7

Prices: £46.00-£48.00 per double room per night, breakfast included
Cheques/cash accepted

Open: Year round except Christmas

Description: A large Victorian house, seven guest rooms and private parking. The ideal location for Warwick Castle, Stratford and the Cotswolds.

Facilities: Rooms:
General: **P**

WARWICK

Shrewley Pools Farm

★★★★Guest Accommodation

Haseley, Warwick, CV35 7HB

SILVER AWARD

T: +44 (0) 1926 484315
E: cathydodd@hotmail.com
W: s-h-systems.co.uk/hotels/shrewley.html

Bedrooms: 2

Prices: £35.00-£50.00 per double room per night, breakfast included
Cheques/cash, euros accepted

Open: Year round except Christmas

Description: Traditional mid-17thC beamed farmhouse set in an acre of gardens on a mixed farm. Five miles north of Warwick on the A4177.

Facilities: Rooms:
General: **P**
Leisure:

WARWICK

Warwick Lodge Guesthouse

★★★Guesthouse

82 Emscote Road, Warwick, CV34 5QJ

T: +44 (0) 1926 492927

Bedrooms: 20

Prices: £22.00-£24.00 per double room per night, room only

Open: Year round

Description: Edwardian period townhouse offering quality B&B accommodation within easy walking distance of Warwick Castle. Ample off-road parking. Maximum age for child: 12 years, Maximum age for infant: Five years.

Facilities: Rooms:
General: **P**

WARWICK

Westham Guesthouse ★★★Guest Accommodation

76 Emscote Road, Warwick, CV34 5QG

T:	+44 (0) 1926 491756
E:	westham.house@ntlworld.com
W:	smoothhound.co.uk/hotels/westham.html
Bedrooms:	8
Prices:	£44.00-£48.00 per double room per night, breakfast included
Open:	Year round
Description:	Comfortable family-run guesthouse situated within a mile of Warwick Castle and on main tourist route.
Facilities:	Rooms: General: **P**

ASHBOURNE

Reevsmoor ★★★★B&B

Hoargate Lane, Hollington, Ashbourne, DE6 3AG

T:	+44 (0) 1335 330318
W:	smoothhound.co.uk
Bedrooms:	2
Prices:	£48.00-£56.00 per double room per night, breakfast included
Open:	Year round
Description:	Small, friendly family B&B in quiet village with comfortable ground floor rooms. Good hearty breakfast, Excellent base for touring, Non-smokers only and country pubs serving meals within walking distance. Short breaks available.
Facilities:	Rooms: General: **P**

BELPER

Hill Top Farm B&B ★★★★B&B

Hill Top Farm, 80 Ashbourne Road, Belper, DE56 2LF

T:	+44 (0) 1773 550338
Bedrooms:	2
Prices:	£23.00 per double room per night, breakfast included
Open:	Year round
Description:	A charming, detached farmhouse in a superb setting with breathtaking views. Ideally situated for visiting local attractions including Crich Tramway Village, Alton Towers, American Adventure and Carsington Water.
Facilities:	Rooms: General: **P**

BURTON-ON-TRENT

Meadowview ♦♦♦Guest Accommodation

203 Newton Road, Winshill, Burton-on-Trent, DE15 0TU

T:	+44 (0) 1283 564046
E:	cllr-pat-hancox@freeola.com
Bedrooms:	2
Prices:	£44.00-£50.00 per twin room per night, breakfast included
Open:	Year round
Description:	Double-fronted detached house with large attractive garden, overlooking River Trent. Property built in 1912.
Facilities:	Rooms: General:

BURTON-ON-TRENT

Redmoor Accommodation ♦♦♦Guest Accommodation

6 Redmoor Close, Winshill, Burton-on-Trent, DE15 0HZ

T:	+44 (0) 1283 531977
E:	petervyze@btinternet.com
Bedrooms:	4
Prices:	£45.00-£50.00 per double room per night, breakfast included Euros accepted
Open:	Year round
Description:	Redmoor accommodation is within five minutes' drive from Burton centre. A quiet cul-de-sac and private off-street parking is available.
Facilities:	Rooms: General: P

CASTLE DONINGTON

Scot's Corner Guesthouse ♦♦♦Guest Accommodation

82 Park Lane, Castle Donington, DE74 2JG

T:	+44 (0) 1332 811226
E:	linda.deary@ntlworld.com
W:	scots-corner.com
Bedrooms:	3
Prices:	£42.00 per double room per night, breakfast included
Open:	Year round
Description:	A warm welcome awaits you in this centrally heated, detached house with a lovely garden and conservatory.
Facilities:	Rooms: General:

DERBY

Braeside Guesthouse ♦♦♦♦Guest Accommodation

113 Derby Road, Risley, Derby, DE72 3SS

T: +44 (0) 115 939 5885
E: bookings@braesideguesthouse.co.uk
W: braesideguesthouse.co.uk

Bedrooms: 6

Prices: £45.00-£60.00 per double room per night, breakfast included
Debit/credit card accepted

Open: Year round

Description: The enthusiastic hosts of this delightful property offer a friendly, personal welcome to guests. Luxurious bedrooms are adjacent to the main house in characterful barn conversions.

Facilities: General: **P**

DERBY

Chuckles Guesthouse ♦♦♦Guest Accommodation

48 Crompton Street, Derby, DE1 1NX

T: +44 (0) 1332 367193
E: ian@chucklesguesthouse.co.uk
W: chucklesguesthouse.co.uk

Bedrooms: 4

Prices: £42.00 per double room per night, breakfast included

Open: Year round

Description: In Derby city centre, Chuckles is a small guesthouse offering warm and inviting surroundings coupled with exceptional quality and service at an affordable price.

Facilities: Rooms:
General:

DERBY

Grace Guesthouse ♦Guest Accommodation

1063 London Road, Alvaston, Derby, DE24 8PZ

T: +44 (0) 1332 571051

Bedrooms: 10

Prices: £40.00 per double room per night, breakfast included

Open: Year round

Description: Clean, comfortable and friendly family-run guesthouse. Home from home. Parking available. Garden at rear. Within easy reach of Derby city centre and the National Forest.

Facilities: General: **P**

DERBY

Green Gables
★★★Guesthouse

19 Highfield Lane, Chaddesden, Derby, DE21 6PG

T:	+44 (0) 1332 672298
E:	enquiries@greengablesuk.co.uk
W:	greengablesuk.co.uk
Bedrooms:	7
Prices:	£27.50-£32.00 per double room per night, breakfast included
Open:	Year round
Description:	A warm welcome to all who stay in our family-run home for holiday or business guests. Quiet location but close to all amenities. City centre approximately one mile away.
Facilities:	General: P

DERBY

International Hotel
★★★Hotel

288 Burton Road, Derby, DE23 6AD

T:	+44 (0) 1332 369321
E:	info@international-hotel.co.uk
W:	international-hotel.co.uk
Bedrooms:	62
Prices:	£45.00-£105.00 per double room per night, breakfast included Debit/credit card, euros accepted
Open:	Year round
Description:	An independently owned hotel and restaurant providing high levels of comfort and service in a friendly atmosphere. Situated 0.5 miles from city centre, ideally located for exploring the Peak District.
Facilities:	Rooms: General: P X

DERBY

Ivy House Farm
♦♦♦♦Guest Accommodation

Stanton-By-Bridge, Derby, DE73 7HT — SILVER AWARD

T:	+44 (0) 1332 863152
E:	mary@guesthouse.fsbusiness.co.uk
W:	house-farm.com
Bedrooms:	6
Prices:	£48.00 per double room per night, breakfast included Debit/credit card accepted
Open:	Year round
Description:	The purpose-built B&B has two upstairs rooms and four ground floor rooms. In the quiet hamlet but close to lots of interesting attractions – Donington Park Racing, Calke Abbey, Alton Towers, Twycross Zoo and Swadlincote Ski Slopes.
Facilities:	General: P Leisure: U

DERBY

Rose and Thistle ♦♦♦Guest Accommodation

21 Charnwood Street, Derby, DE1 2GU

T:	+44 (0) 1332 344103
Bedrooms:	8
Prices:	£40.00-£50.00 per twin room per night, breakfast included
Open:	Year round
Description:	High standard Victorian guesthouse just five minutes from the city centre and rail station. Recently refurbished. Quality accommodation open all year round for bookings.
Facilities:	Call for details

DERBY

Thames House ♦♦♦♦Guest Accommodation

6 Thames Close, Mackworth, Derby, DE22 4HT

T:	+44 (0) 1332 513526
E:	j.swarbrooke@ntlworld.com
Bedrooms:	3
Prices:	£27.50-£30.00 per double room per night, breakfast included
Open:	Year round
Description:	Large, detached property in quiet cul-de-sac. Convenient for city centre and exploring Derbyshire's beautiful countryside. Restaurants to suit all tastes locally – off-road parking.
Facilities:	General: **P**

DERBY

The Lawns Hotel ♦♦♦Guest Accommodation

High Street, Chellaston, Derby, DE73 1TB

T:	+44 (0) 1332 701553
Bedrooms:	24
Prices:	£48.00-£55.00 per double room per night, breakfast included Debit/credit card accepted
Open:	Year round
Description:	The Lawns is warm and inviting with oak beams and its hand-crafted thatch overhanging, L-shaped carvery and drinks bar with comfortable accommodation reasonably priced.
Facilities:	General: **P**

COVENTRY

RIPLEY

Hellinside ★★B&B

1/3 Whitegates, Codnor, Ripley, DE5 9QD

T: +44 (0) 1773 742750
E: hellinside@aol.com

Bedrooms: 2

Prices: £20.00-£23.00 per double room per night, breakfast included

Open: Year round

Description: Detached family home in small village. Private lounge with open fire. Use of computer and internet. Parking available. Convenient for local attractions and public transport.

Facilities: Rooms:
General:

DURHAM

CHESTER LE STREET

Lilac Cottage ★★B&B

Wheatley Well Lane, Plawsworth, Chester Le Street, DH2 3LD

T: +44 (0) 1913 712969

Bedrooms: 3

Prices: £35.00 per double room per night, breakfast included
Cheques/cash accepted

Open: Year round except Christmas

Description: Stone-built Georgian house, fully centrally heated. Four miles from Durham City, three miles from Chester-le-Street.

Facilities: Rooms:
General: P

CHESTER LE STREET

Malling House ♦♦♦Guest Accommodation

1 Oakdale Terrace, Newfield, Chester Le Street, DH2 2SU

T: +44 (0) 1913 702571
E: heather@mallingguesthouse.freeserve.co.uk
W: mallingguesthouse.freeserve.co.uk

Bedrooms: 3

Prices: £48.00-£56.00 per twin room per night, breakfast included
Cheques/cash accepted

Open: Seasonal opening

Description: Friendly accommodation overlooking Sustrans Cycle and Walking Country. Within two miles of county cricket and Beamish. Within six miles of Durham and Metro Centre shopping.

Facilities: Rooms:
General: P
Leisure:

DURHAM

12 The Avenue

♦♦♦Guest Accommodation

Durham, Durham, DH1 4ED

T: +44 (0) 1913 841020
E: janhanim@aol.com

Bedrooms: 2

Prices: £40.00-£42.00 per double room per night, breakfast included

Open: Year round

Description: Victorian terraced family home, eight minutes' walk from the city centre. Convenient on-street parking (Pay parking zone). Near to bus and train stations. Room may be used as a double, twin or triple, bathrooms/shower rooms not en suite.

Facilities: Rooms:
General:

DURHAM

Burnhope Lodge

♦♦♦Guest Accommodation

1 Wrights Way, Burnhope, Durham, DH7 0DL

T: +44 (0) 1207 529596

Bedrooms: 3

Prices: £39.00-£50.00 per twin room per night, breakfast included
Debit/credit card, cheques/cash accepted

Open: Year round except Christmas and New Year

Description: Stay in a relaxing, family-run guesthouse with TV/DVD, tea-/coffee-making facilities, en suite facilities private parking, non-smoking rooms. Open all year.

Facilities: Rooms: TV CDP
General: P

DURHAM

Hamsteels Hall

★★★★Farmhouse

Hamsteels Lane, Quebec, Durham, DH7 9RS

T: +44 (0) 1207 520388
E: june@hamsteelshall.co.uk
W: hamsteelshall.co.uk

Bedrooms: 5

Prices: £40.00-£50.00 per double room per night, breakfast included
Cheques/cash accepted

Open: Seasonal opening

Description: Serviced accommodation in an historical building with four-poster beds, en suite facilities and panoramic views. Ideal for country walks, cycling or touring. Only 10 minutes' drive from Durham City and 15 minutes' drive from Beamish.

Facilities: Rooms: TV
General: P
Leisure:

DURHAM

Ivesley ♦♦♦♦Guest Accommodation

Ivesley, Waterhouses, Durham, DH7 9HB

T:	+44 (0) 1913 734324
E:	ivesley@msn.com
W:	ridingholidays-ivesley.co.uk
Bedrooms:	5
Prices:	£49.00-£64.00 per double room per night, breakfast included Debit/credit card, cheques/cash, euros accepted
Open:	Year round – closed Christmas
Description:	Once a hunting lodge. Avenue planted in 1350s and recently extended to give lovely views. Established, comprehensively equipped equestrian centre. Large indoor and outdoor schools, show jumping hacking and cross country fences.
Facilities:	Rooms: General: Leisure:

DURHAM

Kings Head Hotel ★★★Guest Accommodation

Station Road, Lanchester, Durham, DH7 0EX

T:	+44 (0) 1207 520054
Bedrooms:	6
Prices:	£39.95 per double room per night, room only Debit/credit card accepted
Open:	Seasonal opening – check for details
Description:	A newly refurbished six-bedroom hotel, all with en suite facilities.Fully licensed restaurant and bar.
Facilities:	Rooms: General:

DURHAM

Moorcroft B&B ♦♦♦Guest Accommodation

Moor End Terrace, Belmont, Durham, DH1 1BJ

T:	+44 (0) 1913 867677
E:	moorcroft.dur@hotmail.co.uk
Bedrooms:	2
Prices:	£46.00-£56.00 per double room per night, breakfast included
Open:	Seasonal opening – contact for details
Description:	A family-run Edwardian house near to the centre of the historic city of Durham, offering a warm and friendly welcome.
Facilities:	Rooms: General:

DURHAM

Nafferton Farm ♦♦♦♦Guest Accommodation

Brancepeth, Brancepeth, Durham, DH7 8EF

T:	+44 (0) 1913 780538
E:	sndfell@aol.com
W:	nafferton-farm.co.uk
Bedrooms:	2
Prices:	£35.00-£50.00 per double room per night, breakfast included Cheques/cash, euros accepted
Open:	Seasonal opening – contact for details
Description:	Late 17thC farmhouse in rural location. Spacious bedrooms with en suite facilities panoramic views. Ten minutes from Durham City. Ample parking.
Facilities:	Rooms: General: P Leisure:

DURHAM

Prince Bishop Guesthouse ♦♦♦Guest Accommodation

1 Oxford Terrace, Bowburn, Durham, DH6 5AX

T:	+44 (0) 1913 778703
E:	enquiries@durhamguesthouse.co.uk
W:	durhamguesthouse.co.uk
Bedrooms:	4
Prices:	£45.00-£48.00 per double room per night, breakfast included Debit/credit card, cheques/cash accepted
Open:	Seasonal opening
Description:	Small, family-run, guesthouse. Warm, friendly atmosphere. All rooms have en suite facilities. Excellent home-cooked food, off-road parking.
Facilities:	Rooms: TV General: P

DURHAM

St Johns College ★★Guest Accommodation

3 South Bailey, Durham, DH1 3RJ

T:	+44 (0) 1913 343877
E:	s.l.hobson@durham.ac.uk
W:	durham.ac.uk/st-johns.college
Bedrooms:	45
Prices:	£46.00-£53.00 per twin room per night, breakfast included Debit/credit card, cheques/cash accepted
Open:	Seasonal opening – contact for details
Description:	Located in the heart of Durham City alongside the cathedral, St John's offers accommodation in distinctive, historic buildings with riverside gardens.
Facilities:	Rooms: General:

DURHAM

The Avenue Inn ♦♦Guest Accommodation

Avenue Street, High Shincliffe, Durham, DH1 2PT

T: +44 (0) 1913 865954
E: info@theavenue.biz

Bedrooms: 8

Prices: £40.00-£90.00 per twin room per night, breakfast included
Debit/credit card accepted

Open: Seasonal opening

Description: Cosy village inn with eight bedrooms, mainly en suite. Real ales and a friendly atmosphere.

Facilities: Rooms:
General: P
Leisure:

DURHAM

Van Mildert College (Tunstall Stairs) ★★★Guest Accommodation

Mill Hill Lane, Durham, DH1 3LH

T: +44 (0) 1913 347100
E: van-mildert.college@durham.ac.uk
W: dur.ac.uk/VanMildert/Conferences/

Bedrooms: 30

Prices: £35.00 per twin room per night, room only
Debit/credit card accepted

Open: Seasonal opening – contact for details

Description: College and conference centre in beautiful lakeside surroundings. Adjacent to golf course, 0.75 miles from cathedral and castle – World Heritage site. Closed Easter 2007.

Facilities: Rooms:
General: P
Leisure:

STANLEY

Bushblades Farm ★★★Farmhouse

Tantobie, Harperly, Stanley, DH9 9UA

T: +44 (0) 1207 232722

Bedrooms: 2

Prices: £48.00 per double room per night, breakfast included

Open: Seasonal opening – contact for details

Description: Comfortable Georgian farmhouse situated in rural setting. Within easy reach of Durham City, Beamish Museum, A1(M), Metro Centre and Roman Wall.

Facilities: Rooms:
General: P

STANLEY

Harperley Hotel
♦♦♦Guest Accommodation

Harperley, Stanley, DH9 9TY

T: +44 (0) 1207 234011
E: harperley-hotel@supanet.com

Bedrooms: 5

Prices: £48.00-£55.00 per double room per night, breakfast included
Debit/credit card, cheques/cash accepted

Open: Seasonal opening

Description: Converted granary on the outskirts of Stanley, in the country park area close to the old watermill.

Facilities: Rooms:
General:
Leisure:

STOCKON-ON-TEES

Todds House Farm
★★★Guest Accommodation

Sedgefield, Stockton-On-Tees, TS21 3EL

T: +44 (0) 1740 620244
E: mail@toddshousefarm.co.uk
W: toddshousefarm.co.uk

Bedrooms: 2

Prices: £45.00 per double room per night, breakfast included
Cheques/cash, euros accepted

Open: Seasonal opening – contact for details

Description: Todds House is a small, mixed farm pleasantly situated on a country lane within easy reach of village amenities.

Facilities: Rooms:
General: P

TRIMDON

Polemonium Plantery
★★★★B&B

28 Sunnyside Terrace, Trimdon Grange, Trimdon Station, TS29 6HF

T: +44 (0) 1429 881529
E: bandb@polemonium.co.uk
W: polemonium.co.uk

Bedrooms: 3

Prices: £45.00-£60.00 per double room per night, breakfast included

Open: Year round – closed New Year

Description: A peaceful retreat in a small country village with good access to coast and country.

Facilities: Rooms:
General:
Leisure:

EXETER

Busy Bee B&B ★★★Guest Accommodation

Mellifera, Church Road, Whimple, Exeter, EX5 2TF

T: +44 (0) 1404 823019
W: booking@bandbbusybee.co.uk

Bedrooms: 3

Prices: £40.00-£44.00 per double room per night, breakfast included

Open: Year round except Christmas and New Year

Description: Ideal for coast, city, port or airport; private day room with TV; excellent facilities, private parking; transport to and from airport by arrangement.

Facilities: Rooms:
General: P

EXETER

Culm Vale Country House ★★★B&B

Culm Vale, Stoke Canon, Exeter, EX5 4EG

T: +44 (0) 1392 841615
E: culmvale@hotmail.com

Bedrooms: 3

Prices: £40.00-£45.00 per double room per night, breakfast included
Debit/credit card, cheques/cash accepted

Open: Year round

Description: Victorian country house, set in one acre of garden, 3.5 miles from Exeter city centre. Free parking. Ideal touring base. Spacious accommodation.

Facilities: Rooms: TV
General: P
Leisure:

EXETER

Fingle Glen Farm ♦♦♦Guest Accommodation

Fingle Glen Farm, Tedburn St Mary, Exeter, EX6 6AF

T: +44 (0) 1647 61227

Bedrooms: 2

Prices: £40.00-£48.00 per double room per night, breakfast included

Open: Year round except Christmas and New Year

Description: Warm and friendly welcome. Central for coast and moors with panoramic views. Adjacent to an 18-hole golf course, 0.25 miles from the A30 and five miles from Exeter.

Facilities: Rooms: TV
General: P
Leisure:

EXETER

Great Cummins Farm ★★★★Guest Accommodation

Tedburn St Mary, Exeter, EX6 6BJ

T: +44 (0) 1647 61227
E: davidgaraway@yahoo.co.uk

Bedrooms: 2

Prices: £30.00-£45.00 per double room per night, breakfast included
Euros accepted

Open: Seasonal opening – contact for details

Description: Farm B&B – one splendid double room with private bath. Extra twin-bedded room sharing bathroom for family/group.

Facilities: Rooms:
General: P
Leisure:

EXETER

Hayne Barton Milverton Country Holidays ♦♦Guest Accommodation

Whitestone, Exeter, EX4 2JN

T: +44 (0) 1392 811268
E: g_milverton@hotmail.com
W: milvertoncountryholidays.com

Bedrooms: 2

Prices: £44.00-£50.00 per double room per night, breakfast included
Cheques/cash accepted

Open: Year round

Description: Hayne Barton (Grade II Listed) dating from c1086 (Domesday Book). Sixteen acres of gardens, woodlands and fields. Four miles from Exeter Cathedral. Close to Dartmoor and Torbay.

Facilities: Rooms: TV
General: P
Leisure: U

EXETER

Home Farm ★★★★Farmhouse

Farringdon, Exeter, EX5 2HY

T: +44 (0) 1395 232293

Bedrooms: 3

Prices: £46.00-£52.00 per double room per night, breakfast included
Cheques/cash, euros accepted

Open: Year round except Christmas and New Year

Description: Farmhouse in rural position with plenty of space and yummy breakfasts. Convenient for M5, Exeter University and Westpoint.

Facilities: Rooms: TV
General: P
Leisure:

EXETER

Lower Thornton Farm ♦♦♦♦Guest Accommodation

Kenn, Exeter, EX6 7XH

T: +44 (0) 1392 833434
E: will@willclack.plus.com

Bedrooms: 3

Prices: £46.00-£50.00 per double room per night, breakfast included
Cheques/cash, euros accepted

Open: Year round

Description: Relax at our secluded family farm with panoramic views. Two miles A38. Easy access to Exeter, Torquay, Dartmoor and the coast.

Facilities: Rooms:
General:
Leisure:

EXETER

Road Lodge ★★★Guest Accommodation

East Wonford Lodge, 42 East Wonford Hill, Exeter, EX1 3TF

T: +44 (0) 1392 438200
E: exeter@roadlodge.co.uk
W: roadlodge.co.uk

Bedrooms: 8

Prices: £30.00-£45.00 per double room per night, breakfast included
Debit/credit card, cheques/cash accepted

Open: Year round except Christmas and New Year

Description: Georgian B&B only four minutes from Exeter airport; free hot tub and parking.

Facilities: Rooms:
General:
Leisure:

EXMOUTH

Victoria Guesthouse ★★★★Guesthouse

131 Victoria Road, Exmouth, EX8 1DR SILVER AWARD

T: +44 (0) 1395 222882
E: aw@exmouth.net
W: exmouth.net

Bedrooms: 3

Prices: £46.00-£58.00 per double room per night, breakfast included
Cheques/cash, euros accepted

Open: Year round except Christmas and New Year

Description: Hotel standards of comfort in the personal, friendly atmosphere of a small guesthouse only yards from the beach and marina.

Facilities: Rooms:
General:

NEWTON ABBOTT

Great Doccombe Farm ♦♦♦♦Guest Accommodation

Doccombe, Moretonhampstead, Newton Abbot, TQ13 8SS

T:	+44 (0) 1647 440694
E:	david.oakey3@btopenworld.com
W:	greatdoccombefarm.co.uk
Bedrooms:	2
Prices:	£22.00-£24.00 per double room per night, breakfast included Cheques/cash accepted
Open:	Year round except Christmas and New Year
Description:	Lovely, old Listed farmhouse in Dartmoor National Park. Comfortable accommodation, good home-cooking. Ideal centre for walking, riding, fishing and exploring Dartmoor.
Facilities:	Rooms: General: P

BLAYDON-ON-TYNE

A1 Hedgefield House ★★★Guest Accommodation

Stella Road, Blaydon-on-Tyne, NE21 4LR

T:	+44 (0) 1914 137373
E:	david@hedgefieldhouse.co.uk
W:	hedgefieldhouse.co.uk
Bedrooms:	11
Prices:	£40.00-£80.00 per double room per night, breakfast included Debit/credit card accepted
Prices:	Year round
Description:	Stunning Georgian residence in three acres of wooded gardens. Peaceful yet situated two miles from Gateshead shopping centre and Newcastle city centre.
Facilities:	Rooms: General: P Leisure:

CONSETT

St Ives B&B ★★B&B

22 St Ives Road, Leadgate, Consett, DH8 7PY

T:	+44 (0) 1207 580173
Bedrooms:	2
Prices:	£25.00 per person per night, breakfast included
Open:	Year round Closed New Year
Description:	Two family-sized rooms with en suites. Central to Newcastle, Durham and Weardale. Adjacent to the coast-to-coast cycle track.
Facilities:	Rooms: General:

GATESHEAD

The Bewick Hotel ★★★Guesthouse

145 Prince Consort Road, Gateshead, NE8 4DS

T: +44 (0) 1914 771809
E: bewickhotel@hotmail.com
W: bewickhotel.co.uk

Bedrooms: 13

Prices: £46.00 per double room per night, breakfast included
Debit/credit card, cheques/cash accepted

Open: Seasonal opening

Description: The priority at Bewick Hotel is to provide guests with the kind of personal and professional attention which has established its name as the perfect place to stay when visiting Gateshead or Newcastle for business or pleasure.

Facilities: Rooms:
General:

NEWCASTLE UPON TYNE

Albatross ★★Hostel

51 Grainger Street, Newcastle upon Tyne, NE1 5JE

T: +44 (0) 1912 331330
E: info@albatrossnewcastle.co.uk
W: albatrossnewcastle.com

Bedrooms: 24

Prices: £16.50-£23.50 per person per night, room only
Debit/credit card, cheques/cash accepted

Open: Year round

Description: International backpackers hostel/budget accommodation for individual travellers and groups.

Facilities: Rooms:
General:

NEWCASTLE UPON TYNE

Avenue Hotel ♦♦♦Guest Accommodation

2 Manor House Road, Jesmond, Newcastle upon Tyne, NE2 2LU

T: +44 (0) 1912 811396
E: avenue.hotel@amserve.com

Bedrooms: 11

Prices: £49.50-£55.00 per double room per night, breakfast included
Debit/credit card, cheques/cash accepted

Open: Year round except Christmas

Description: The Avenue Hotel is a small friendly, family-type hotel within a mile of the city centre.

Facilities: Rooms:
General:

NEWCASTLE UPON TYNE

Greenholme ★★★B&B

40 South View, East Denton, Newcastle upon Tyne, NE5 2BP

T:	+44 (0) 1912 674828
E:	info@greenholmeguesthouse.co.uk
W:	greenholmeguesthouse.co.uk
Bedrooms:	2
Prices:	£46.00 per double room per night, breakfast included
Open:	Year round except Christmas and New Year
Description:	Greenholme is a family-run B&B specifically targeted at travellers who to not wish to stay at large, impersonal hotels and like to be pampered.
Facilities:	Rooms: General: Leisure:

NEWCASTLE UPON TYNE

Houghton North Farm ★★★★Hostel

Heddon On The Wall, Newcastle Upon Tyne, NE15 0EZ

T:	+44 (0) 1661 854364
E:	wjlaws@btconnect.com
W:	hadrianswallaccommodation.com
Bedrooms:	6
Prices:	£22.00-£40.00 per person per night, breakfast included Debit/credit card accepted
Open:	Seasonal opening – contact for details
Description:	Private hostel comprising six bunk bedrooms, two en suite, with fitted kitchen, lounge and drying facilities. Adjacent to Hadrian's Wall.
Facilities:	Rooms: General:

NEWCASTLE UPON TYNE

Newcastle YHA ★★Hostel

107 Jesmond Road, Newcastle upon Tyne, NE2 1NJ

T:	+44 (0) 1912 812570
E:	newcastle@yha.org.uk
W:	yha.org.uk
Bedrooms:	18
Prices:	£17.50-£42.00 per person per night, breakfast included Debit/credit card, cheques/cash,euros accepted
Open:	Seasonal opening – contact for details
Description:	A large townhouse located close to city centre. Within reach of Hadrian's Wall and Durham Cathedral.
Facilities:	Rooms: General: Leisure:

NEWCASTLE UPON TYNE

Northumbria University ★★★Campus

Claude Gibb Hall and Camden Court, University Precinct, Northumberland Road, Newcastle upon Tyne, NE1 8SG

T:	+44 (0) 1912 274024
E:	rc.conferences@northumbria.ac.uk
W:	northumbria.ac.uk/conferences
Bedrooms:	518
Prices:	£23.25-£39.50 per person per night, breakfast included Debit/credit card, cheques/cash accepted
Open:	Seasonal opening – contact for details
Description:	Claude Gibb Hall and Camden Court are both three star city centre halls of residence close to all the nightlife, shopping and attractions in Newcastle upon Tyne.
Facilities:	Rooms: General: P

NEWCASTLE UPON TYNE

Stonehaven Lodge ★★★Guesthouse

Prestwick Road Ends, Ponteland, Newcastle Upon Tyne, NE20 9BX

T:	+44 (0) 1661 872363
E:	brenanderson@ncletw.freeserve.co.uk
W:	stonehavenlodge.co.uk
Bedrooms:	3
Prices:	£40.00-£50.00 per double room per night, breakfast included Euros accepted
Open:	Seasonal opening – contact for details
Description:	Stone building, semi-facing the Cheviots on the Prestwick roundabout, on the A696 to Jedburgh. Two hundred yards past Newcastle Airport.
Facilities:	Rooms: TV General: P

SOUTH SHIELDS

Ainsley Guesthouse ★★★Guesthouse

59 Ocean Road, South Shields, NE33 2JJ

T:	+44 (0) 1914 543399
E:	info@ainsleyguesthouse.co.uk
W:	ainsleyguesthouse.co.uk
Bedrooms:	6
Prices:	£42.00 per double room per night, breakfast included
Open:	Year round – closed New Year
Description:	Victorian, three-storey terraced townhouse retaining many original features. Clean, well appointed, tastefully decorated rooms. Emphasis on good service and friendly atmosphere.
Facilities:	Rooms: TV General:

SOUTH SHIELDS

Atlantis Guesthouse ★★★Guesthouse

55 Ocean Road, South Shields, NE33 2JJ

T: +44 (0) 1914 556070
E: atlantisguesthouse@btopenworld.com
W: atlantisguesthouse.com

Bedrooms: 7

Prices: £40.00-£50.00 per double room per night, breakfast included
Cheques/cash, euros accepted

Open: Year round

Description: Atlantis is ideal for pleasure and business. Friendly service. Family run. Newly renovated. All rooms en suite. Close to Roman fort and Bede's World as well as the town centre and the seafront.

Facilities: Rooms:
General:

SOUTH SHIELDS

Beaches Guesthouse ♦♦♦Guest Accommodation

81 Ocean Road, South Shields, NE33 2JJ

T: +44 (0) 1914 563262
E: jdocchar@yahoo.co.uk
W: smoothhound.com

Bedrooms: 5

Prices: £45.00 per double room per night, breakfast included
Cheques/cash, euros accepted

Open: Year round except Christmas and New Year

Description: Comfortable guesthouse, recently refurbished. Centrally located for parks, beaches and shopping. All rooms en suite, video/TV, DVDs, hairdryers, coolers.

Facilities: Rooms:
General:

SOUTH SHIELDS

Britannia Guesthouse ♦♦♦♦Guest Accommodation

54/56 Julian Avenue, South Shields, NE33 2EW

T: +44 (0) 1914 560896
E: cbgh56@hotmail.com
W: britanniaguesthouse.com

Bedrooms: 10

Prices: £48.00-£52.00 per double room per night, breakfast included
Debit/credit card, cheques/cash, euros accepted

Open: Seasonal opening

Description: Beautiful Victorian house. Very close to beaches, town centre and transport. Very spacious en suite rooms, tea-/coffee-making facilities and Sky TV.

Facilities: Rooms:
General: P

SOUTH SHIELDS

Clifton Guesthouse ★★★Guest Accommodation

101 Ocean Road, South Shields, NE33 2JL

T: +44 (0) 1914 551965
E: info@thecliftonguesthouse.com
W: thecliftonguesthouse.com

Bedrooms: 8

Prices: £40.00-£50.00 per double room per night, breakfast included
Debit/credit card, cheques/cash, euros accepted

Open: Year round Closed New Year

Description: Family-run B&B located in the centre of South Shields, within good reach of local attractions.

Facilities: Rooms:
General:

SOUTH SHIELDS

Forest Guesthouse ★★★★Guesthouse

117 Ocean Road, South Shields, NE33 2JL

T: +44 (0) 1914 548160
E: enquiries@forestguesthouse.com
W: forestguesthouse.com

Bedrooms: 6

Prices: £45.00-£50.00 per double room per night, breakfast included
Debit/credit card, cheques/cash, euros accepted

Open: Seasonal opening

Description: Small, friendly, relaxed atmosphere. Rooms have video or DVD, Sky and Freeview. Central heating, showers in all rooms. En suite available. Tea/coffee-making facilities. Play Station available, video library, fridges, hairdryers and shavers.

Facilities: Rooms:
General: P

SOUTH SHIELDS

Marina Guesthouse ★★★Guest Accommodation

32 Sea View Terrace, South Shields, NE33 2NW

T: +44 (0) 1914 561998
E: austin@marina32.fsnet.co.uk

Bedrooms: 3

Prices: £40.00-£60.00 per double room per night, breakfast included

Open: Year round except Christmas and New Year

Description: A Victorian terraced house overlooking South Marine park with panoramic views along the coast.

Facilities: Rooms:
General:

SOUTH SHIELDS

The Magpies Nest ♦♦♦Guest Accommodation

75 Ocean Road, South Shields, NE33 2JJ

T: +44 (0) 1914 552361
E: Christine.Taylor3@btinternet.com
W: magpies-nest.co.uk

Bedrooms: 7

Prices: £44.00 per twin room per night, breakfast included
Debit/credit card, euros accepted

Open: Seasonal opening – contact for details

Description: Seven-bedroomed guesthouse in South Shields, five minutes from parks, beaches and nightlife. Sunderland and Newcastle bus and metro links nearby.

Facilities: Rooms:
General:

WASHINGTON

George Washington Golf & Country Club ★★★Hotel

Stone Cellar Road, High Usworth, Washington, NE37 1PH

T: +44 (0) 870 609 6173
E: reservations@georgewashington.co.uk
W: georgewashington.co.uk

Bedrooms: 103

Prices: £49.00-£84.00 per double room per night, breakfast included
Debit/credit card, cheques/cash, euros accepted

Open: Seasonal opening

Description: Set in a tranquil area within its own grounds, yet easily accessible by all major routes. The hotel is perfect for business or pleasure.

Facilities: Rooms:
General:
Leisure:

WHITLEY BAY

The Glen Esk Guesthouse ★★★Guesthouse

8 South Parade, Whitley Bay, NE26 2RG

T: +44 (0) 1912 530103
E: info@glenesk-guesthouse.co.uk
W: glenesk-guesthouse.co.uk

Bedrooms: 11

Prices: £40.00-£60.00 per twin room per night, breakfast included
Cheques/cash accepted

Open: Seasonal opening – contact for details

Description: Centrally located for pubs, clubs and restaurants our rooms have satellite TV, tea-/coffee-making, showers. Stag, hen and commercial guests.

Facilities: Rooms:
General:
Leisure:

BARTON-UPON-HUMBER

West Wold Farmhouse ♦♦♦♦Guest Accommodation

West Wold Farmhouse, Deepdale, Barton-upon-Humber, DN18 6ED

T:	+44 (0) 1652 633293
E:	westwoldfarm@aol.com
Bedrooms:	2
Prices:	£44.00 per double room per night, breakfast included
Open:	Year round
Description:	Small, friendly, comfortable, family farmhouse, offering the Great British breakfast; hearty, home-cooked meals, freshly prepared using local quality produce.
Facilities:	Rooms: General:

BEVERLEY

6 St Mary's Close ♦♦♦Guest Accommodation

St Mary's Close, Beverley, HU17 7AY

T:	+44 (0) 1482 868837
E:	da@ytb.org.uk
Bedrooms:	2
Prices:	£17.00-£20.00 per single room per night, breakfast included
Open:	Seasonal opening – contact for details
Description:	Friendly and quality accommodation. Close to town centre and all amenities, but situated in a quiet residential part of Beverley. Warm welcome assured.
Facilities:	Rooms: General:

BEVERLEY

Beck View Guesthouse ★★★★Guest Accommodation

1a Blucher Lane, Beverley, HU17 0PT

T:	+44 (0) 1482 882332
E:	BeckViewHouse@aol.com
W:	beckviewguesthouse.co.uk
Bedrooms:	5
Prices:	£40.00-£50.00 per double room per night, breakfast included Debit/credit card, euros accepted
Open:	Year round
Description:	Beck View House is a large, modern bungalow with off-road parking. Offering high-quality accommodation in a warm and friendly atmosphere.
Facilities:	Rooms: General: Leisure:

BEVERLEY

Eastgate Guesthouse ★★★★Guest Accommodation

7 Eastgate, Beverley, HU17 0DR

T: +44 (0) 1482 868464

Bedrooms: 16

Prices: £30.00-£65.00 per double room per night, breakfast included
Euros accepted

Open: Year round

Description: Eastgate is a Victorian guesthouse, established and run by the same family for 30 years. Close to the town centre, Beverley Minster and railway station.

Facilities: Rooms:
General:

BEVERLEY

St Mary's Terrace ★★★B&B

16 St Mary's Terrace, Beverley, HU17 8EH

T: +44 (0) 1482 860608

Bedrooms: 2

Prices: £40.00-£50.00 per double room per night, breakfast included

Open: Year round

Description: Victorian terraced accommodation conveniently situated a few minutes' walk from the centre of historic Beverley. Private entrance and private sitting room.

Facilities: Rooms:
General:

BEVERLEY

The Inn on the Bar

8 North Bar Without, Beverley, HU17 7AA

T: +44 (0) 1482 868137
E: da@ytb.org.uk

Bedrooms: 4

Prices: £35.00-£50.00 per double room per night, room only
Debit/credit card accepted

Open: Year round

Description: The Inn on the Bar is a friendly, family-run hotel in one of Beverley's finest buildings, close to all shops, bars and restaurants. All rooms en suite or with private bathroom.

Facilities: Rooms:
General:
Leisure:

BEVERLEY

Westfield B&B ★★B&B

13 Westfield Avenue, Beverley, HU17 7HA

T:	+44 (0) 1482 860212
Bedrooms:	2
Prices:	£36.00-£40.00 per twin room per night, breakfast included
Open:	Seasonal opening – contact for details
Description:	Quality accommodation in quiet road, 10 minutes' walk to town centre. Good amenities for tourists and all home-cooked food.
Facilities:	Rooms: General:

BROUGH

Green Dragon Hotel ★★★★Inn

Cowgate, Welton, Brough, HU15 1NB

T: **E:**	+44 (0) 1482 666700 da@ytb.org.uk
Bedrooms:	10
Prices:	£49.50 per double room per night, breakfast included
Open:	Year round
Description:	A 17thC inn on the Yorkshire Wolds in the centre of the picturesque conservation village of Welton.
Facilities:	Rooms: General: Leisure:

COTTINGHAM

Newholme ♦♦♦Guest Accommodation

47 Thwaite Street, Cottingham, HU16 4QX

T:	+44 (0) 1482 849879
Bedrooms:	5
Prices:	£28.00-£44.00 per double room per night, breakfast included Euros accepted
Open:	Seasonal opening – contact for details
Description:	Newholme is a friendly, family-run B&B with all the luxuries of home.Guest lounge with Sky TV and large comfortable sofas. All rooms have TV and tea-/coffee-making facilities.
Facilities:	Rooms: General:

HULL

Acorn Guesthouse ♦♦♦Guest Accommodation

719 Beverley Road, Hull, HU6 7JN

T: +44 (0) 1482 853248
E: please@call.above.number.uk

Bedrooms: 9

Prices: £40.00 per double room per night, breakfast included

Open: Year round

Description: City centre penthouse suite. Two double bedrooms, wonderful views over Queens Gardens. Five minutes' walk to bus and train station.

Facilities: Rooms:
General: P

HULL

Allandra Hotel ♦♦♦Guest Accommodation

5 Park Avenue, Princes Avenue, Hull, HU5 3EN

T: +44 (0) 1482 493349
E: macklin2003@macklin2003.karoo.co.uk

Bedrooms: 23

Prices: £34.00-£39.00 per double room per night, breakfast included
Debit/credit card,euros accepted

Open: Year round

Description: A delightful townhouse hotel situated in an historic conservation area.

Facilities: Rooms:
General: P

HULL

Cornerbrook Guesthouse ★★★★Guest Accommodation

1 Desmond Avenue, Beverley Road, Hull, HU6 7JY

T: +44 (0) 1482 474272
E: jackie@cornerbrook.freeserve.co.uk

Bedrooms: 5

Prices: £44.00 per double room per night, breakfast included

Open: Seasonal opening – contact for details

Description: The luxurious Cornerbrook guesthouse has been graded four stars for quality and superior customer care. This B&B is non-smoking throughout for your comfort, and is family owned. It is two miles from Hull city centre.

Facilities: Rooms:
General: P
Leisure:

HULL

The Admiral Guesthouse ★★★B&B

234 The Boulevard, Hull, HU3 3ED

T:	+44 (0) 1482 329664
Bedrooms:	3
Prices:	£30.00 per double room per night, breakfast included
Open:	Seasonal opening – contact for details
Description:	The guesthouse is in a conservation area. The building is a spacious, late Victorian, former vicarage.
Facilities:	Rooms: General: P

HULL

The Earlsmere Hotel ★★★Guesthouse

76-78 Sunny Bank, Hull, HU3 1LQ

T: **E:** **W:**	+44 (0) 1482 341977 su@earlsmerehotel.karoo.co.uk earlsmerehotel.karoo.net
Bedrooms:	10
Prices:	£43.75 per double room per night, breakfast included
Open:	Year round
Description:	The Earlsmere Hotel has modernised rooms upgraded to a high standard awaiting the discerning guest. It is a mile from the city centre and The Deep museum.
Facilities:	Rooms: General:

NORTH FERRIBY

B&B @103 ★★★B&B

103 Ferriby High Road, North Ferriby, HU14 3LA

T: **E:** **W:**	+44 (0) 1482 633637 info@bnb103.co.uk bnb103.co.uk
Bedrooms:	4
Prices:	£40.00-£50.00 per double room per night, breakfast included Euros accepted
Open:	Seasonal opening – contact for details
Description:	B&B @ 103 is convenient for Humber Bridge, Hull and Beverley. York is 45 minutes by car. Private dwelling, large garden, view of River Humber and off-road parking.
Facilities:	Rooms: General: P

ULCEBY

Thornton Hunt Inn
★★★★Inn

Main Street, Thornton Curtis, Ulceby, DN39 6XW

T: +44 (0) 1469 531252
E: peter@thornton-inn.co.uk
W: thornton-inn.co.uk

Bedrooms: 6

Prices: £47.95 per double room per night, room only
Debit/credit card accepted

Open: Year round

Description: Family-run Grade II Listed building with traditional bar meals available lunch and evenings. Convenient for airport, Humber Bridge M180.

Facilities: Rooms:
General: P
Leisure:

LEICESTER

Abinger Guesthouse
★★★Guesthouse

175 Hinckley Road, Leicester, LE3 0TF

T: +44 (0) 116 255 4674
E: bobwel1234@aol.com
W: leicesterguest.co.uk

Bedrooms: 8

Prices: £48.00-£52.00 per double room per night, breakfast included
Debit/credit card, euros accepted

Open: Year round

Description: Guesthouse rates, hotel quality. We are proud of our rating and treat all guests like hotel inspectors!

Facilities: Rooms:
General:

LEICESTER

Croft Hotel
★★★Guesthouse

3 Stanley Road, Leicester, LE2 1RF

T: +44 (0) 116 270 3220
E: crofthotel@hotmail.com
W: crofthotel-web.co.uk

Bedrooms: 25

Prices: £45.00-£60.00 per double room per night, breakfast included
Debit/credit card accepted

Open: Year round

Description: Well located near Leicester city centre, University of Leicester, De Montford Hall and Victoria Park. The Croft is ideal for commercial people, visitors, students and their parents and music lovers as well.

Facilities: Rooms:
General: P

LEICESTER

Glenfield Lodge Hotel ★Guest Accommodation

4 Glenfield Road, Leicester, LE3 6AP

T: +44 (0) 116 262 7554
E: glenleic@aol.com
W: glenfieldlodge.co.uk

Bedrooms: 8

Prices: £48.00 per double room per night, breakfast included
Euros accepted

Open: Year round

Description: A small, friendly budget hotel with an interesting ornamental courtyard.

Facilities: Rooms:
General: P

LEICESTER

Three Ways Farm ♦♦♦Guest Accommodation

Melton Road, Queniborough, Leicester, LE7 3FN

T: +44 (0) 116 260 0472

Bedrooms: 3

Prices: £48.00-£56.00 per double room per night, breakfast included

Open: Year round

Description: A warm welcome awaits you in this tastefully decorated bungalow with comfortable beds.

Facilities: General: P
Leisure:

LOUGHBOROUGH

Highbury Guesthouse ♦♦♦Guest Accommodation

146 Leicester Road, Loughborough, LE11 2AQ

T: +44 (0) 1509 230545
E: irene@thehighburyguesthouse.co.uk
W: thehighburyguesthouse.co.uk

Bedrooms: 7

Prices: £47.00 per double room per night, breakfast included
Debit/credit card, euros accepted

Open: Year round

Description: Well run family guesthouse conservatory dining room, car park for off-road parking surrounded by well kept gardens.

Facilities: Rooms:
General: P

LEICESTER

Holywell House
★★Guesthouse

Leicester Road, Loughborough, LE11 2AG

T: +44 (0) 1509 267891
E: lezanddez@holywell.here.co.uk
W: holywell.here.co.uk

Bedrooms: 3

Prices: £45.00 per double room per night, breakfast included
Debit/credit card accepted

Open: Year round

Description: Holywell House is a late 17thC townhouse close to the centre of the main market square of Loughborough.

Facilities: Rooms:
General:

LEICESTER

LOUGHBOROUGH

Garendon Park Hotel
★★★Guesthouse

92 Leicester Road, Loughborough, LE11 2AQ

T: +44 (0) 1509 236557
E: info@garendonparkhotel.co.uk
W: morningtonweb.com/garendon

Bedrooms: 4

Prices: £49.00 per double room per night, breakfast included
Debit/credit card accepted

Open: Year round

Description: Victorian building near to town centre. Great Central Railway just around the corner.

Facilities: Rooms:
General:
Leisure:

LINCOLN

Aaron Whisby Guesthouse
★★★Guesthouse

262 West Parade, Lincoln, LN1 1LY

T: +44 (0) 1522 526930
E: dianajones@aaronwhisby.fsnet.co.uk

Bedrooms: 1

Prices: £45.00-£50.00 per double room per night, breakfast included
Debit/credit card accepted

Open: Year round

Description: B&B within close proximity to university, high street and cathedral quarter.

Facilities: General: **P**

LINCOLN

LINCOLN

Hamilton Hotel ★★Guest Accommodation

2 Hamilton Road, Lincoln, LN5 8ED

T:	+44 (0) 1522 528243
W:	hamiltonhotel.co.uk
Bedrooms:	9
Prices:	£45.00-£55.00 per double room per night, breakfast included Debit/credit card, cheques/cash accepted
Open:	Year round
Description:	Detached hotel with well-preserved Victorian character. Close to Lincoln city centre, spacious parking.
Facilities:	Rooms: General: P

LINCOLN

Manor Farm Stables ♦♦♦♦Guest Accommodation

Broxholme, Lincoln, LN1 2NG

T:	+44 (0) 1522 704220
E:	pfieldson@lineone.net
W:	rfarmstables.co.uk
Bedrooms:	1
Prices:	£45.00-£50.00 per double room per night, breakfast included
Open:	Year round except Christmas and New Year
Description:	Our 19thC barn conversion offers a private ground floor suite (bedroom, lounge, dining room, bathroom) just six miles from Lincoln.
Facilities:	Rooms: General: P Leisure:

LINCOLN

Newport Cottage ♦♦♦♦Guest Accommodation

Newport Cottage, 21 Newport, Lincoln, LN1 3DQ

T:	+44 (0) 1522 534470
Bedrooms:	3
Prices:	£45.00-£60.00 per double room per night, breakfast included Cheques/cash accepted
Open:	Year round
Description:	Detached period home set in secluded grounds close to cathedral, castle, and bailgate area. All rooms en suite with secure parking.
Facilities:	Rooms: General: P

LINCOLN

Robindale

★★★★B&B

Back Lane, Brattleby, Lincoln, LN1 2SQ

T:	+44 (0) 1522 730712
Bedrooms:	2
Prices:	£38.00-£44.00 per double room per night, breakfast included
Open:	Year round except Christmas
Description:	Rural, family home, six miles to Lincoln. Tea/coffee, TV lounge, conservatory, garden and car parking. Lincolnshire Showground and Hemswell Antiques close by.
Facilities:	Rooms: General: P

LINCOLN

Swanside

♦♦♦♦Guest Accommodation

Saxilby Road, Odder, Lincoln, LN1 2BB

T:	+44 (0) 1522 704797
E:	swanside-lincoln@btopenworld.com
Bedrooms:	2
Prices:	£40.00-£44.00 per double room per night, breakfast included
Open:	Year round except Christmas
Description:	A small guesthouse with two rooms both en suite.
Facilities:	Rooms: General: P

LINCOLN

The Old Vicarage

★★★★Guest Accommodation

East Street, Nettleham, Lincoln, LN2 2SL

T:	+44 (0) 1522 750819
E:	susan@oldvic.net
Bedrooms:	2
Prices:	£50.00 per double room per night, breakfast included
Open:	Year round except Christmas and New Year
Description:	Georgian house near the centre of attractive village, with traditional "Green" and "Beck". Local pubs serve meals. Comfortable rooms, full English breakfast. Frequent buses to Lincoln.
Facilities:	Rooms: General: P

LINCOLN

The Wren Guesthouse
★★★Guesthouse

22 St Catherines, Lincoln, LN5 8LY

T: +44 (0) 1522 537949
E: kateatthewren@aol.com
W: wrenguesthouse.co.uk

Bedrooms: 3

Prices: £40.00-£45.00 per twin room per night, breakfast included
Euros accepted

Open: Year round except Christmas

Description: Family-run guesthouse. All rooms with tea-/coffee-making facilities, TV and central heating, some with en suite. Friendly service and parking.

Facilities: Rooms:
General: P

LINCOLN

Welbeck Cottage
★★★★B&B

19 Meadow Lane, South Hykeham, Lincoln, LN6 9PF

T: +44 (0) 1522 692669
E: mad@wellbeck1.demon.co.uk

Bedrooms: 3

Prices: £40.00 per double room per night, breakfast included
Cheques/cash accepted

Open: Year round

Description: Two double, one twin en suite rooms in quiet rural location. Friendly, personal service.

Facilities: Rooms:
General: P

LINCOLN

Wheelwrights Cottage
★★★★B&B

Haddington, Lincoln, LN5 9EF

T: +44 (0) 1522 788154
E: dawn.dunning2@btopenworld.com

Bedrooms: 2

Prices: £40.00 per double room per night, breakfast included

Open: Year round except Christmas and New Year

Description: Situated in a small hamlet, south of Lincoln. Friendly welcome. Patio and large garden. Independent access to ground floor accommodation.

Facilities: Rooms:
General: P

WADDINGTON

Carnforth Guesthouse

★★★★Guesthouse

Carnforth, Tinkers Lane, Waddington, LN5 9RU

T:	+44 (0) 1522 722492
E:	mail@carnforthguesthouse.co.uk
W:	carnforthguesthouse.co.uk
Bedrooms:	1
Prices:	£35.00-£50.00 per double room per night, breakfast included
Open:	Year round
Description:	A friendly, family-run, non-smoking guesthouse within easy reach of historic Lincoln's city centre, ample parking available.
Facilities:	Rooms: General: P

LINCOLN

BIRKENHEAD

Villa Venezia

♦♦♦Guest Accommodation

14-16 Prenton Road West, Birkenhead, CH42 9PN

T:	+44 (0) 151 608 9212
Bedrooms:	7
Prices:	£41.50 per double room per night, breakfast included Debit/credit card accepted
Open:	Year round
Description:	The Villa Venezia is a comfortably furnished hotel situated in Central Birkenhead, close to all amenities and housing one of Wirral's most popular Italian restaurants.
Facilities:	Rooms: TV General: P

LIVERPOOL

LIVERPOOL

A Church View Guesthouse

★★B&B

7 Church Avenue, Liverpool, L9 4SG

T:	+44 (0) 151 525 8166
Bedrooms:	2
Prices:	£33.00 per double room per night, room only
Open:	Year round except Christmas and New Year
Description:	Small guesthouse close to Aintree's racecourse and station. Easy access to M57, M58 and Liverpool and Everton football clubs. Six miles to city centre.
Facilities:	Rooms: TV General: P

LIVERPOOL

Blenheim Lodge

37 Aigburth Drive, Liverpool, L17 4JE

T:	+44 (0) 151 727 7380
Bedrooms:	17
Prices:	£35.00-£50.00 per double room per night, breakfast included Debit/credit card, cheques/cash accepted
Open:	Year round
Description:	Large Victorian villa overlooking Sefton Park, offering first-class B&B accommodation at an unbeatable price. Former family home of The Beatles' Stu Sutcliffe.
Facilities:	Rooms: General:

LIVERPOOL

Bounty House ★★★★Guesthouse

Church Avenue, Liverpool, L9 4SG

T:	+44 (0) 151 281 6750
Bedrooms:	6
Prices:	£40.00-£70.00 per double room per night, breakfast included Debit/credit card, cheques/cash, euros accepted
Open:	Seasonal opening – contact for details
Description:	Bounty House offers quality en suite accommodation, wheelchair-friendly bedroom with en suite. Attractive menu. Guests can enjoy indoor, heated pool/ sauna.
Facilities:	Rooms: General: Leisure:

LIVERPOOL

Holme-Leigh Guesthouse ♦♦♦Guest Accommodation

93 Woodcroft Road, Liverpool, L15 2HG

T:	+44 (0) 151 734 2216
E:	info@holmeleigh.com
W:	holmeleigh.com
Bedrooms:	11
Prices:	£38.00 per double room per night, breakfast included Debit/credit card, cheques/cash accepted
Open:	Year round
Description:	A Victorian guesthouse in a residential area close to Sefton Park and Picton Leisure Centre within easy walking distance.
Facilities:	Rooms: General:

WALLASEY

Sea Level Hotel ★★Guesthouse

126 Victoria Road, Wallasey, CH45 9LD

T:	+44 (0) 151 639 3408
Bedrooms:	14
Prices:	£35.00-£45.00 per double room per night, breakfast included Debit/credit card, cheques/cash, euros accepted
Open:	Year round except Christmas and New Year
Description:	Homely, family-run hotel offering a warm welcome and wholesome food. Light meals available until 22:00.
Facilities:	Rooms: General: **P**

BEXLEY

66 Arcadian Avenue ★★★Guest Accommodation

66 Arcadian Avenue, Bexley, DA5 1JW

T:	+44 (0) 20 8303 5732
Bedrooms:	2
Prices:	£30.00-£55.00 per twin room per night, breakfast included
Open:	Year round except Christmas and New Year
Description:	B&B accommodation in two twin-bedded rooms with private facilities. Private off-street parking.
Facilities:	Rooms: General: **P**

BEXLEY

Blendon Lodge ★★★★Guest Accommodation

30 Blendon Road, Bexley, DA5 1BW

T:	+44 (0) 20 8303 2571
Bedrooms:	3
Prices:	£30.00-£35.00 per double room per night, room only Cheques/cash accepted
Open:	Year round
Description:	Very friendly family home. Bungalow so good for elderly people. Refurbished. Within walking distance of two pubs with good food, and Bexley Village with many different kinds of food.
Facilities:	Rooms: General: **P**

ILFORD

Cranbrook Hotel ♦♦Guest Accommodation

22-24 Coventry Road, Ilford, IG1 4QR

T:	+44 (0) 20 8554 6544
Bedrooms:	67
Prices:	£45.00-£50.00 per double room per night, breakfast included
Open:	Year round
Description:	The Cranbrook Hotel is ideally situated for business and recreational purposes. The pleasant location allows for easy access to central London and is five minutes from Gants Hill Underground station.
Facilities:	Call for details

KENLEY

Appledore ★★★B&B

6 Betula Close, Kenley, CR8 5ET

T:	+44 (0) 20 8668 4631
Bedrooms:	3
Prices:	£45.00-£50.00 per twin room per night, breakfast included
Open:	Year round
Description:	Modern four-bedroomed detached house in the picturesque village of Kenley.
Facilities:	Rooms: [symbols] General: [symbols]

KINGSTON UPON THAMES

40 The Bittoms ★★B&B

40 The Bittoms, Kingston upon Thames, KT1 2AP

T:	+44 (0) 20 8541 3171
Bedrooms:	2
Prices:	£40.00-£70.00 per double room per night, breakfast included Euros accepted
Open:	Year round
Description:	Easy access to all transports and airports. Near Kingston town centre but in a quiet area. Semi-detached townhouse. En suite bedrooms. Parking available.
Facilities:	Rooms: [symbols] General: P[symbols]

LONDON

8 St Albans Road ♦♦♦Guest Accommodation

8 St Albans Road, Kingston upon Thames, KT2 5HQ

T:	+44 (0) 20 8549 5910
Bedrooms:	4
Prices:	£35.00 per single room per night, breakfast included
Open:	Year round except Christmas and New Year
Description:	A private, detached house in a quiet road. Excellent location near river, town centre and tourist attractions.
Facilities:	Rooms: General: Leisure:

LONDON

8 Yeats Close ★★B&B

Yeats Close, 8 Eliot Park, London, SE13 7ET

T:	+44 (0) 20 8318 3421
E:	pathu@tesco.net
Bedrooms:	3
Prices:	£45.00-£50.00 per double room per night, breakfast included
Open:	Year round
Description:	Homely base in a quiet road, close to Blackheath and Greenwich. With frequent train and Docklands Light Railway (DLR) connections to central London, Kent.
Facilities:	Rooms: General:

LONDON

Abbey Court & Westpoint Hotel

♦♦♦Guest Accommodation

174 Sussex Gardens, London, W2 1TP

T:	+44 (0) 20 7402 0281
E:	info@abbeycourt.com
W:	abbeycourthotel.com
Bedrooms:	102
Prices:	£49.00-£74.00 per double room per night, room only Debit/credit card, cheques/cash accepted
Open:	Year round
Description:	Good value accommodation in central London, with easy access to London's tourist attractions and shopping areas. Within walking distance of Hyde Park. Car parking available.
Facilities:	Rooms: General:

LONDON

Ace Hotel

★★★Hostel

16-22 Gunterstone Road, West Kensington, London, W14 9BX

T: +44 (0) 20 7602 6600
E: reception@ace-hotel.co.uk
W: acehotel.co.uk

Bedrooms: 40

Prices: £15.00-£26.00 per person per night, breakfast included
Debit/credit card, cheques/cash accepted

Open: Year round

Description: Ace Hotel – the newly established budget accommodation in Central London, setting a new standard for budget accommodation in the UK.

Facilities: Rooms:
General:
Leisure:

LONDON

Crofton Park Holdenby

★★B&B

28 Holdenbury Raod, London, SE4 2DA

T: +44 (0) 20 8694 0011
E: savitri.gaines@totalise.co.uk
W: ukhomestay.net

Bedrooms: 2

Prices: £20.00 per single room per night, breakfast included

Open: Year round

Description: Spacious, comfortable, clean, easy access to buses 171, 172, 122, P4 and direct to Crofton Park train station.

Facilities: Rooms:
General:

LONDON

Dover Hotel

★★Guest Accommodation

44 Belgrave Road, London, SW1V 1RG

T: +44 (0) 20 7821 9085
E: reception@dover-hotel.co.uk
W: dover-hotel.co.uk

Bedrooms: 33

Prices: £40.00-£69.00 per twin room per night, breakfast included
Debit/credit card, cheques/cash, euros accepted

Open: Year round

Description: Small, friendly B&B hotel within easy access of all major attractions and three minutes from Victoria station.

Facilities: Rooms:
General:

LONDON

Europa Hotel

♦♦♦Guest Accommodation

62 Anson Road, London, N7 0AA

T: +44 (0) 20 7607 5935
E: info@europahotellondon.co.uk
W: europahotellondon.co.uk

Bedrooms: 33

Prices: £45.00-£49.00 per double room per night, breakfast included
Debit/credit card, cheques/cash accepted

Open: Year round

Description: Easily accessible by Underground and buses. Close to shops and only 15 minutes away from central London.

Facilities: Rooms:
General:

LONDON

Geoffrey B&B

★★B&B

66 Geoffrey Road, Brockley, London, SE4 1NT

T: +44 (0) 20 8691 3887
E: andrea.dechamps@btclick.com

Bedrooms: 2

Prices: £40.00-£48.00 per double room per night, breakfast included

Open: Year round except Christmas

Description: Friendly and relaxed Victorian family home. Enchanting garden. Attractive guest room, cosy beds. Easy links to City/West End.

Facilities: Rooms:
General: P

LONDON

Grange Lodge Hotel

♦♦♦Guest Accommodation

48-50 Grange Road, London, W5 5BX

T: +44 (0) 20 8567 1049
E: enquiries@londonlodgehotels.com
W: activehotels.com

Bedrooms: 14

Prices: £48.00-£59.00 per twin room per night, breakfast included
Debit/credit card, cheques/cash, euros accepted

Open: Year round except Christmas and New Year

Description: Midway between Central London and Heathrow airport, with good Underground links. Home away from home, friendly with an informal atmosphere.

Facilities: Rooms:
General: P

LONDON

Hyde Park Rooms Hotel ★★Guest Accommodation

137 Sussex Gardens, London, W2 2RX

T: +44 (0) 20 7723 0225
E: reception@hydeparkrooms.com
W: hydeparkrooms.com

Bedrooms: 14

Prices: £45.00-£58.00 per double room per night, breakfast included
Debit/credit card, cheques/cash,euros accepted

Open: Year round except Christmas and New Year

Description: Small, family-run, centrally-located hotel. Within walking distance of Hyde Park and Paddington station.
Car parking available.

Facilities: Rooms:
General:
Leisure:

LONDON

M B Guesthouse ★★Guest Accommodation

7 Bolden Street, London, SE8 4JF

T: +44 (0) 20 8692 7030
E: mbguesthouse@yahoo.co.uk

Bedrooms: 3

Prices: £45.00-£55.00 per double room per night, breakfast included

Open: Year round

Description: Listed building in a cul-de-sac. All rooms are bright with central heating, colour TV, own sink and tea-/coffee-making facilities. Full English breakfast available. Two minutes' walk from station for easy access to central London.

Facilities: Rooms:
General: P
Leisure:

LONDON

Marble Arch Inn ★★Guest Accommodation

49-50 Upper Berkeley Street, London, W1H 5QR

T: +44 (0) 20 7723 7888
E: sales@marblearch-inn.co.uk
W: marblearch-inn.co.uk

Bedrooms: 29

Prices: £35.00-£75.00 per double room per night, breakfast included
Debit/credit card, cheques/cash, euros accepted

Open: Year round

Description: Friendly hotel located near Marble Arch, within minutes of Hyde Park and Oxford Street and within easy reach of other major attractions.

Facilities: Rooms:
General:

LONDON

Pane Residence
♦♦Guest Accommodation

154 Boundary Road, London, N22 6AE

T: +44 (0) 20 8889 3735

Bedrooms: 3

Prices: £36.00 per twin room per night, room only
Cheques/cash, euros accepted

Open: Year round

Description: In a pleasant location near Turnpike Lane Underground station on the Piccadilly line and close to Alexandra Palace. Kitchen facilities are available for guests' use.

Facilities: Rooms:
General: P

LONDON

Queens Hotel
♦♦Guest Accommodation

33 Anson Road, London, N7 0RB

T: +44 (0) 20 7607 4725
E: queens@stavrouhotels.co.uk
W: stavrouhotels.co.uk

Bedrooms: 44

Prices: £38.00-£58.00 per double room per night, breakfast included
Debit/credit card, cheques/cash, euros accepted

Open: Year round

Description: Large detached Georgian property easily accessible by Underground and buses. Shops and other amenities nearby. Fifteen minutes to the West End.

Facilities: Rooms:
General: P

LONDON

Stanley House Hotel
★★Guest Accommodation

19-21 Belgrave Road, London, SW1V 1RB

T: +44 (0) 20 7834 5042
E: cmahotel@aol.com
W: londonbudgethotels.co.uk

Bedrooms: 44

Prices: £45.00-£55.00 per double room per night, breakfast included
Debit/credit card, cheques/cash accepted

Open: Year round

Description: Located in elegant Belgravia only a few minutes' walk from Victoria station. Within easy access of London's most famous sights and the West End for theatre and shopping.

Facilities: Rooms:
General:

LONDON

The Corner House
Rating applied for

28 Royal Hill, London, SE10 8RT

T: +44 (0) 20 8692 3023
E: joannacourtney@aol.com

Bedrooms: 4

Prices: £30.00-£65.00 per double room per night, breakfast included
Euros accepted

Open: Year round

Description: In Greenwich conservation area, period property. Near all places of interest, museums, park, river, and antique market.

Facilities: Rooms:
General:

LONDON

The Globetrotter Inn London
★★★★Hostel

Ashlar Court, Ravenscourt Gardens, Stamford Brook, London, W6 0TU

T: +44 (0) 20 8746 3112
E: london@globetrotterinns.com
W: globetrotterinns.com

Bedrooms: 101

Prices: £19.00-£24.00 per person per night, breakfast included
Debit/credit card, cheques/cash, euros accepted

Open: Seasonal opening – contact for details

Description: A former nurses home (architecturally Listed), converted to provide a new standard of superior hostel accommodation in a wonderful location.

Facilities: Rooms:
General: P
Leisure:

LONDON

White Lodge Hotel
★★★Guest Accommodation

1 Church Lane, London, N8 7BU

T: +44 (0) 20 8348 9765
E: info@whitelodgehornsey.co.uk
W: whitelodgehornsey.co.uk

Bedrooms: 16

Prices: £42.00-£50.00 per double room per night, breakfast included
Debit/credit card, cheques/cash accepted

Open: Year round except Christmas

Description: Small, friendly, family hotel offering personal service and easy access to bus and Underground. Located in a North London suburb.

Facilities: Rooms:
General:

ORPINGTON

The Mary Rose Hotel ★Hotel

High Street, Orpington, BR5 3NJ

T:	+44 (0) 1689 871917
E:	info@maryrose.co.uk
W:	maryrose.co.uk
Bedrooms:	40
Prices:	£45.00-£75.00 per double room per night, breakfast included Debit/credit card, cheques/cash accepted
Open:	Year round
Description:	A 16thC inn with modern hotel facilities, 25 minutes by train from Victoria. Chartwell, Leeds and Hever Castles are all within 45 minutes.
Facilities:	Rooms: General:

PINNER

Delcon ★★Guest Accommodation

468 Pinner Road, Pinner, HA5 5RR

T:	+44 (0) 20 8863 1054
E:	delcon@homecall.co.uk
Bedrooms:	2
Prices:	£40.00 per twin room per night, breakfast included
Open:	Year round
Description:	1930s semi-detached family home with own drive and easy reach of the Metropolitan line Underground.
Facilities:	Rooms: General: P

RICHMOND

11 Leyborne Park ★★★★Guest Accommodation

11 Leyborne Park, Richmond, TW9 3HB

T:	+44 (0) 20 8948 1615
E:	mary@stay-in-kew.com
W:	stay-in-kew.com
Bedrooms:	4
Prices:	£35.00-£40.00 per double room per night, breakfast included Cheques/cash, euros accepted
Open:	Year round except Christmas and New Year
Description:	Edwardian house close to Kew Gardens, Public Records Office and with easy access to central London.
Facilities:	Rooms: General: P

RICHMOND

29 West Park Road ★★★★Guest Accommodation

29 West Park Road, Kew, Richmond, TW9 4DA

T: +44 (0) 20 8878 0505
E: aghillman@aol.uk

Bedrooms: 2

Prices: £40.00-£70.00 per double room per night, breakfast included
Euros accepted

Open: Year round except Christmas and New Year

Description: Edwardian house situated near to Kew Gardens and underground station. A quiet location, ideal for visiting London and the south west.

Facilities: Rooms:
General: P

RICHMOND

9 Selwyn Court ★Guest Accommodation

9 Selwyn Court, Church Road, Richmond, TW10 6LR

T: +44 (0) 20 8940 3309

Bedrooms: 1

Prices: £24.00-£35.00 per double room per night, breakfast included
Cheques/cash accepted

Open: Year round except Christmas and New Year

Description: Comfortable double room in a penthouse flat, with lovely views of Richmond. Within easy reach of the station. Bus stop outside.

Facilities: Rooms:

RICHMOND

Ivy Cottage ♦♦♦Guest Accommodation

Upper Ham Road, Richmond, TW10 5LA

T: +44 (0) 20 8940 8601
E: taylor@dbta.freeserve.co.uk
W: dbta.freeserve.co.uk

Bedrooms: 4

Prices: £30.00-£50.00 per double room per night, breakfast included

Open: Year round

Description: Charming, Virginia creeper-clad Georgian home, offering exceptional views over Ham Common. Period features dating from 1760. Garden. Accommodation available for single and family occupancy. Safe parking and good bus route.

Facilities: Rooms:
General:

RICHMOND

West Park Gardens ★★★Guest Accommodation

105 Mortlake Road, Richmond, TW9 4AA

T: +44 (0) 20 8876 6842
E: nj.edwards@ukonline.co.uk

Bedrooms: 1

Prices: £40.00-£60.00 per twin room per night, breakfast included

Open: Year round

Description: Warm welcome is extended. Victorian house. Near Kew Gardens Underground. National Archives (PRO) three minutes' walk. Off-street parking nearby. The suite is available as a single or twin.

Facilities: Rooms:
General: P

SOUTH CROYDON

Ginetta Guesthouse ★★★Guest Accommodation

32 Rylandes Road, South Croydon, CR2 8EA

T: +44 (0) 20 8657 3132

Bedrooms: 6

Prices: £26.00 per double room per night, breakfast included

Open: Year round

Description: Near to the countryside and all amenities. Semi-detached property offering three double rooms and three single rooms. One of the double rooms and two of the single rooms have en suite facilities.

Facilities: Rooms:
General: P

SOUTH CROYDON

Owlets ★★★B&B

112 Arundel Avenue, South Croydon, CR2 8BH

T: +44 (0) 20 8657 5213

Bedrooms: 3

Prices: £45.00-£48.00 per twin room per night, breakfast included
Cheques/cash, euros accepted

Open: Year round

Description: Friendly, family-run establishment in a quiet location. Convenient for buses to Croydon and central London by train. Car service available by arrangement.

Facilities: Rooms:
General:

SURBITON

The Broadway Lodge ♦♦Guest Accommodation

41 The Broadway, Tolworth, Surbiton, KT6 7DJ

T: +44 (0) 20 8399 6555
E: info@broadwaylodge.co.uk

Bedrooms: 8

Prices: £42.00 per double room per night, breakfast included
Debit/credit card, cheques/cash accepted

Open: Seasonal opening – contact for details

Description: New clean and cosy B&B. Next to Tolworth Tower. Two miles from Kingston shopping centre and Hampton Court.

Facilities: Rooms:
General:

SURBITON

Villiers Lodge B&B ★★B&B

1 Cranes Park, Surbiton, KT5 8AB

T: +44 (0) 20 8399 6000

Bedrooms: 3

Prices: £35.00 per twin room per night, breakfast included
Cheques/cash, euros accepted

Open: Year round

Description: Villiers Lodge is a large, detached house in a quiet residential road very close to excellent bus and train services.

Facilities: Rooms:
General: P

TEDDINGTON

King Edwards Grove ★★★Guest Accommodation

King Edwards Grove, Teddington, TW11 9LY

T: +44 (0) 20 8977 7251

Bedrooms: 2

Prices: £30.00-£50.00 per twin room per night, breakfast included

Open: Year round except Christmas and New Year

Description: Friendly home in a quiet Edwardian road. Close to Teddington Studios, the Thames and Hampton Court. Bus to Twickenham and Heathrow. Only 35 minutes to central London by train.

Facilities: Rooms:
General:

TWICKENHAM

Avalon Cottage
★★★Guest Accommodation

50 Moor Mead Road, Twickenham, TW1 1JS

T:	+44 (0) 20 8744 2178
E:	avaloncottage@anftel.com
W:	avalon-cottage.com
Bedrooms:	3
Prices:	£40.00-£60.00 per double room per night, room only Cheques/cash, euros accepted
Open:	Year round
Description:	Avalon Cottage is a private Edwardian house in St Margarets, overlooking a park and tennis courts. Twenty minutes to Waterloo by train.
Facilities:	Rooms: General: P Leisure:

LONDON

ALTRINCHAM

Cobweb Cottage
★★★B&B

110 Hale Road, Altrincham, WA15 9HJ

T:	+44 (0) 161 928 3675
Bedrooms:	2
Prices:	£40.00-£46.00 per double room per night, breakfast included
Open:	Year round except Christmas and New Year
Description:	Charming Victorian Cottage.
Facilities:	Rooms: General:

MANCHESTER

BOLTON

Highgrove Guesthouse
★★★Guesthouse

63 Manchester Road, Bolton, BL2 1ES

T:	+44 (0) 1204 384928
E:	thehighgrove@btconnect.com
W:	highgroveguesthouse.co.uk
Bedrooms:	12
Prices:	£45.00 per double room per night, breakfast included Debit/credit card accepted
Open:	Year round
Description:	Modern, quality accommodation.
Facilities:	Rooms: General: P Leisure:

BOLTON

Morden Grange Guesthouse ◆◆◆Guest Accommodation

15 Chadwick Street, The Haulgh, Bolton, BL2 1JN

T:	+44 (0) 1204 522000
E:	enquiries@mordengrange.co.uk
W:	mordengrange.co.uk
Bedrooms:	7
Prices:	£38.00 per twin room per night, breakfast included
Open:	Seasonal opening – contact for details
Description:	Large Victorian family-run guesthouse.
Facilities:	Rooms: General:

MANCHESTER

Britannia Airport Hotel ★★Hotel

Palatine Road, Northenden, Manchester, M22 4FH

T:	+44 (0) 161 455 0166
E:	res720@britanniahotels.com
W:	britanniahotels.com
Bedrooms:	325
Prices:	£45.00-£70.00 per double room per night, room only Debit/credit card, cheques/cash, euros accepted
Open:	Year round
Description:	This modern, purpose-built hotel has easy access to the motorway network. Manchester Airport is only three miles distant and a shuttle bus operates on a regular timetable. Manchester City Centre, The Trafford Centre and the universities are all within 15 minutes' drive.
Facilities:	Rooms: General:

MANCHESTER

Lancashire County Cricket Club & Old Trafford Lodge Guest Accommodation rating applied for

Talbot Road, Old Trafford, Manchester, M16 0PX

T:	+44 (0) 161 874 3333
E:	lodge@lccc.co.uk
W:	lccc.co.uk
Bedrooms:	56
Prices:	£49.00-£69.00 per double room per night, breakfast included Debit/credit card accepted
Open:	Year round except Christmas and New Year
Description:	Superb 68-bedroom development, situated at Old Trafford Cricket Ground. All the rooms are en suite. The executive rooms have their own balcony. Five minutes from Manchester city centre.
Facilities:	Rooms: General:

MANCHESTER

Luther King House ♦♦♦Guest Accommodation

Brighton Grove, Wilmslow Road, M14 5JP

T: +44 (0) 161 224 6404

Bedrooms: 46

Prices: £44.00 per double room per night, breakfast included
Debit/credit card, cheques/cash, euros accepted

Open: Year round except Christmas and New Year

Description: Luther King House is set in two acres of grounds, in a tree-lined suburb of south Manchester. This unique location offers peace and tranquillity, yet is only a short distance from the city centre.

Facilities: Rooms:
General:
Leisure:

MANCHESTER

Stay Inn Hotel ♦♦♦Guest Accommodation

55 Blackfriars Road, Salford, M3 7DB

T: +44 (0) 161 907 2277
E: info@stayinn.co.uk
W: stayinn.co.uk

Bedrooms: 105

Prices: £49.50-£55.00 per double room per night, room only
Debit/credit card accepted

Open: Year round

Description: Purpose-built hotel.

Facilities: Rooms:
General:

MANCHESTER

The Hatters ★Hostel

50 Newton Street, Manchester, M1 2EA

T: +44 (0) 161 236 9500
E: manchester@hattersgroup.com
W: hattersgroup.com

Bedrooms: 15

Prices: £14.50-£30.00 per person per night, room only
Debit/credit card, cheques/cash accepted

Open: Year round

Description: City centre hostel providing central, secure, warm and friendly service. Located close to rail and bus stations in a Listed building.

Facilities: Rooms:
General:
Leisure:

STOCKPORT

Britannia Hotel – Stockport ★★Hotel

67 Dialstone Lane, Offerton, Stockport, SK2 6AG

T: +44 (0) 161 930 1000
E: res702@britanniahotels.com
W: britanniahotels.com

Bedrooms: 180

Prices: £39.00-£65.00 per double room per night, room only
Debit/credit card, cheques/cash accepted

Open: Year round

Description: A modern hotel in a quiet residential district close to Stockport's bustling town centre with its wide range of shops and entertainment. There is also an attractive leisure centre with pool.

Facilities: Rooms:
General:
Leisure:

STOCKPORT

Curzon House ♦♦♦Guest Accommodation

3 Curzon Road, Heald Green, Cheadle, Stockport, SK8 3LN

T: +44 (0) 161 436 2804
E: curzonhouse@aol.com
W: smoothhound.co.uk

Bedrooms: 3

Prices: £35.00-£45.00 per double room per night, breakfast included

Open: Year round except Christmas and New Year

Description: Friendly B&B accommodation.

Facilities: Rooms:
General:

MANCHESTER

Spring Cottage ♦♦♦Guest Accommodation

60 Hulme Hall Road, Cheadle Hulme, Stockport, SK8 6JZ

T: +44 (0) 161 485 1037

Bedrooms: 9

Prices: £49.00 per double room per night, breakfast included
Debit/credit card accepted

Open: Year round except Christmas and New Year

Description: A delightfully maintained period house.

Facilities: Rooms:
General: P

BAWBURGH

Old Lodge
♦♦♦♦Guest Accommodation

New Road, Bawburgh, NR9 3LZ
SILVER AWARD

T: +44 (0) 1603 742798
E: peggy@theoldlodge.freeserve.co.uk
W: theoldlodge.co.uk

Bedrooms: 2

Prices: £40.00-£44.00 per twin room per night, room only

Open: Year round

Description: Four diamond, silver award. Non-smoking. Norwich outskirts. Rural aspect. Quiet, attractive accommodation. All en suite. Four-poster bed.

Facilities: Rooms:
General: **P**

COLTISHALL

Hedges Guesthouse
★★★★Guest Accommodation

Tunstead Road, Coltishall, NR12 7AL

T: +44 (0) 1603 738361
E: info@hedgesbandb.co.uk
W: hedgesbandb.co.uk

Bedrooms: 3

Prices: £48.00 per twin room per night, room only

Open: Year round

Description: Small, licensed B&B in 1.5 acres of grounds, surrounded by open countryside. En suite rooms. Close to Norwich, Norfolk Broads and coast.

Facilities: Rooms:
General: **P**

HELLESDON

Cairdean
★★★★B&B

71 Middletons Lane, Hellesdon, NR6 5NS

T: +44 (0) 1603 419041
E: info@cairdean.co.uk
W: cairdean.co.uk

Bedrooms: 2

Prices: £42.00 per twin room per night, room only

Open: Year round

Description: Large, comfortable, non-smoking, quiet bungalow with off-road parking. All rooms are en suite or private bathroom.

Facilities: Rooms:
General: **P**

NORWICH

58 Norwich Road

★★★★B&B

Norwich Road, Wroxham, Norwich, NR12 8RX

T:	+44 (0) 1603 783998
Bedrooms:	1
Prices:	£45.00 per double room per night, breakfast included
Open:	Seasonal opening – contact for details
Description:	Double bedroom with private bathroom in a small, friendly B&B 50 yards from the Broads at Wroxham.
Facilities:	Rooms: General: **P** Leisure:

NORWICH

Aylwyne House

★★★Guest Accommodation

59 Aylsham Road, Norwich, NR3 2HF

T:	+44 (0) 1603 665798
E:	aylwyne@firenet.uk.net
W:	tiscover.co.uk/gb/guide/5gb,en/objectId,ACC15597gb/home.html
Bedrooms:	3
Prices:	£46.00 per twin room per night, room only
Open:	Year round
Description:	Non-smoking establishment. Modern family home overlooking parks and within easy walking distance of city and cathedral.
Facilities:	Rooms: General: **P**

NORWICH

Driftwood Lodge

★★★B&B

102 Wroxham Road, Sprowston, Norwich, NR7 8EX

T:	+44 (0) 1603 444908
E:	info@driftwoodlodge.co.uk
W:	driftwoodlodge.co.uk
Bedrooms:	2
Prices:	£45.00-£60.00 per twin room per night, breakfast included
Open:	Year round
Description:	Standing in its own grounds, 1930s brick guesthouse offers a warm welcome. Large secure car parking, well lit at night. Garage for bikes.
Facilities:	Rooms: General: **P**

NORWICH

Edmar Lodge ★★★Guest Accommodation

64 Earlham Road, Norwich, NR2 3DF

T: +44 (0) 1603 615599
E: mail@edmarlodge.co.uk
W: edmarlodge.co.uk

Bedrooms: 5

Prices: £40.00-£65.00 per double room per night, breakfast included

Open: Year round

Description: Welcoming smile, friendly service, every comfort together with a wonderful breakfast that sets you up for the day.

Facilities: Rooms:
General: **P**

NORWICH

Majority Cottage ♦♦♦♦Guest Accommodation

Wymondham Road, East Carleton, Norwich, NR14 8JB GOLD AWARD

T: +44 (0) 1508 571198
E: richardphillips@majority.freeserve.co.uk
W: tiscover.co.uk/gb/guide/5gb,en/objectId,ACC19350gb/home.html

Bedrooms: 2

Prices: £35.00-£50.00 per twin room per night, room only

Open: Year round

Description: Grade II Listed cottage, ideally suited so you are able to enjoy all the fine county of Norfolk has to offer.

Facilities: Rooms:
General: **P**

NORWICH

Old Corner Shop Guesthouse ★★★B&B

26 Cromer Road, Norwich, NR6 6LZ

T: +44 (0) 1603 419000
E: info@theoldcornershopguesthouse.co.uk
W: theoldcornershopguesthouse.co.uk

Bedrooms: 4

Prices: £42.00 per twin room per night, room only

Open: Year round

Description: A family-run guesthouse with four en suite bedrooms. Private car park.

Facilities: Rooms:
General: **P**

RACKHEATH

Barn Court ★★★Guest Accommodation

6 Back Lane, Rackheath, NR13 6NN

T:	+44 (0) 1603 782536
E:	barncourtbb@hotmail.com
W:	tiscover.co.uk/gb/guide/5gb,en/objectId,ACC15603gb/home.html
Bedrooms:	3
Prices:	£48.00-£55.00 per double room per night, breakfast included
Open:	Year round
Description:	Five miles from Norwich, with its castle, museums, market, excellent shopping and leisure facilities and two miles from the heart of the Norfolk Broads at Wroxham. A homely atmosphere within a bungalow, built around a courtyard, which was converted from a 17thC stable block.
Facilities:	Rooms: General:

SOUTH WALSHAM

Leeward B&B ★★★★Guest Accommodation

5 Broad Lane, South Walsham, NR13 6EE

T:	+44 (0) 1603 270491
E:	a.horsfield@tiscali.co.uk
W:	te.wanadoo-members.co.uk/stayawhileinnorfolk
Bedrooms:	1
Prices:	£45.00-£55.00 per double room per night, breakfast included
Open:	Year round
Description:	Detached bungalow on a quiet lane just 10 minutes' walk from the water, situated in a pretty Broadland village.
Facilities:	Rooms: General: P

WROXHAM

Wroxham Park Lodge ★★★★B&B

142 Norwich Road, Wroxham, NR12 8SA

T:	+44 (0) 1603 782991
E:	parklodge@computer-assist.net
W:	wroxhamparklodge.com
Bedrooms:	3
Prices:	£48.00-£58.00 per double room per night, breakfast included
Open:	Year round
Description:	Comfortable Victorian house with lovely garden. Half a mile from Wroxham broads/centre. Central for all broads and Norfolk attractions.
Facilities:	Rooms: General: P

NOTTINGHAM

The Grove Guesthouse ♦♦♦Guest Accommodation

8 Grove Street, Beeston, Nottingham, NG9 1JL

T: +44 (0) 115 925 9854

Bedrooms: 6

Prices: £40.00-£44.00 per double room per night, room only
Cheques/cash accepted

Open: Year round except Christmas and New Year

Description: A small, friendly, Victorian guesthouse, close to QMC, Siemens, Boots, the university and the tennis centre. Jct 25 of the M1 is four miles away; East Midlands Airport is six.

Facilities: Rooms:
General: **P**

NOTTINGHAM

Vine Lodge ♦♦♦♦Guest Accommodation

8 Highbury Road, Keyworth, Nottingham, NG12 5JB

T: +44 (0) 115 937 3944
E: enquiries@vine-lodge.co.uk
W: vine-lodge.co.uk

Bedrooms: 2

Prices: £35.00-£55.00 per double room per night, breakfast included

Open: Year round

Description: Just seven miles from the centre of Nottingham, Vine Lodge is a comfortable warm home complemented by the friendly welcome from the owners. All rooms have TV, tea-/coffee-making facilities and en suite. A cooked breakfast is provided.

Facilities: Rooms:
General:
Leisure:

ABINGDON

85 Shelley Close ♦♦♦Guest Accommodation

Shelley Close, Abingdon, OX14 1PR

T: +44 (0) 1235 522573

Bedrooms: 2

Prices: £46.00-£48.00 per twin room per night, breakfast included

Open: Year round except Christmas and New Year

Description: One bedroom flat on the ground floor. B&B accommodation.

Facilities: Rooms: TV
General: **P**

ABINGDON

The White House ♦♦Guest Accommodation

Faringdon Road, Shippon, Abingdon, OX13 6LW

T: +44 (0) 1235 521998
E: judymccairns@freeuk.com

Bedrooms: 6

Prices: £45.00-£50.00 per double room per night, breakfast included

Open: Year round

Description: Large, medieval house retaining oak beamed rooms set in an acre of delightful gardens. Very close to Abingdon and A34.

Facilities: Rooms:
General: P

FARINGDON

The Old Rectory ♦♦♦♦Guest Accommodation

Hinton Waldrist, Faringdon, SN7 8SA

T: +44 (0) 1865 821228

Bedrooms: 3

Prices: £45.00-£55.00 per double room per night, breakfast included
Cheques/cash accepted

Open: Year round except Christmas and New Year

Description: Historic Rectory dating from 14thC, offering spacious, comfortable, non-smoking accommodation. Large garden, views to River Thames, excellent local pub food.

Facilities: Rooms:
General: P
Leisure:

KIDLINGTON

Colliers B&B ♦♦♦Guest Accommodation

55 Nethercote Road, Tackley, Kidlington, OX5 3AT

T: +44 (0) 1869 331255
E: colliersbnb@virgin.net
W: colliersbnb.co.uk

Bedrooms: 2

Prices: £25.00-£50.00 per double room per night, breakfast included

Open: Year round

Description: Ground-floor accommodation with off-road parking. Bus and train service. Dogs and horses welcome. Situated in exceptional village with scenic walks and rides. Excellent pub for evening meals.

Facilities: Rooms:
General: P
Leisure:

KIDLINGTON

Home Farm

★★★Farmhouse

Mansmoor Lane, Charlton on Otmoor, Kidlington, OX5 2US SILVER AWARD

T: +44 (0) 1865 331267

Bedrooms: 2

Prices: £40.00-£60.00 per twin room per night, breakfast included

Open: Year round except Christmas and New Year

Description: Modern, working farmhouse, 0.5 miles from village. On sheep and arable farm in quiet location. Full English breakfast served. Pets welcome. Stabling available. Many pubs nearby serving good food. Central to Bicester, Woodstock and Oxford.

Facilities: Rooms:
General: P

OXFORD

21 Lincoln Road

★★★B&B

21 Lincoln Road, Oxford, OX1 4TB

T: +44 (0) 1865 246944
E: gbaleham@hotmail.com

Bedrooms: 2

Prices: £30.00-£35.00 per single room per night, breakfast included
Cheques/cash accepted

Open: Year round except Christmas and New Year

Description: Two quiet single en suite rooms in ground-floor annexe of cosy semi-detached home. Twenty minute walk from centre and convenient for ring roads. Off-street parking.

Facilities: Rooms:
General: P

OXFORD

Arden Lodge

★★★Guest Accommodation

34 Sunderland Avenue, Off Banbury Road, Oxford, OX2 8DX

T: +44 (0) 1865 552076

Bedrooms: 3

Prices: £48.00-£50.00 per double room per night, breakfast included
Cheques/cash accepted

Open: Year round except Christmas and New Year

Description: Modern, detached house in a select area of Oxford. In an excellent position for touring Blenheim Palace, the Cotswolds, Stratford-upon-Avon and London. Close to the river, parks and country inns. Within easy reach city centre.

Facilities: Rooms:
General: P

OXFORD

Becket House
★★Guest Accommodation

5 Becket Street, Oxford, OX1 1PP

T:	+44 (0) 1865 724675
Bedrooms:	9
Prices:	£48.00-£62.00 per double room per night, breakfast included Debit/credit card, cheques/cash accepted
Open:	Year round except Christmas and New Year
Description:	Convenient for the rail and bus stations, city centre and colleges. No car necessary due to central location.
Facilities:	Rooms: General:

OXFORD

Home Farm House
♦♦♦♦Guest Accommodation

Holton, Oxford, OX33 1QA

T: **E:** **W:**	+44 (0) 1865 872334 sonja.barter@tiscali.co.uk homefarmholton.co.uk
Bedrooms:	2
Prices:	£40.00-£70.00 per double room per night, breakfast included
Open:	Year round except Christmas and New Year
Description:	Private country home with well furnished rooms set in 15 acres of historic park land with lake and country garden.
Facilities:	Rooms: General: P Leisure:

OXFORD

Oxford YHA
★★★★Hostel

2a Botley Road, Oxford, OX2 0AB

T: **E:** **W:**	+44 (0) 1865 727275 oxford@yha.org.uk yha.org.uk
Beds:	44
Prices:	£15.95-£20.95 per person per night, room only Debit/credit card, cheques/cash accepted
Open:	Year round
Description:	Brand new, purpose-built YHA, all rooms en suite, offering a friendly service with excellent facilities. Popular with individuals, groups and families.
Facilities:	Rooms: General:

OXFORD

Sportsview Guesthouse ★★★Guest Accommodation

106-110 Abingdon Road, Oxford, OX1 4PX

T:	+44 (0) 1865 244268
E:	stay@sportsview-guest-house.freeserve.co.uk
W:	sportsviewguesthouse.co.uk
Bedrooms:	20
Prices:	£46.00-£68.00 per double room per night, breakfast included Debit/credit card, cheques/cash accepted
Open:	Year round
Description:	A friendly, family-run Victorian house overlooking Queens Sports Grounds ad Boathouse. Situated near the city centre. Rooms furnished and decorated to a high standard.
Facilities:	Rooms: General: P

WITNEY

The Close Guesthouse ♦♦♦Guest Accommodation

Witney Road, Long Hanborough, Witney, OX29 8HF

T:	+44 (0) 1993 882485
Bedrooms:	9
Prices:	£40.00 per double room per night, breakfast included Cheques/cash accepted
Open:	Year round Closed New Year
Description:	Large, detached house, set in 1.5 acres. All rooms purpose-built. On A4095 Witney side of Long Hanborough, Oxford.
Facilities:	Rooms: General: P

PETERBOROUGH

Cobnut Cottage ♦♦♦♦Guest Accommodation

45 Peterborough Road, Castor, Peterborough, PE5 7AX

T:	+44 (0) 1733 380745
E:	enquiries@cobnut-cottage.co.uk
W:	cobnut-cottage.co.uk
Bedrooms:	3
Prices:	£44.00-£52.00 per twin room per night, room only
Open:	Year round
Description:	Stone-built Listed cottage. Low beamed ceilings. Traditionally decorated and furnished. All modern conveniences in warm and friendly period atmosphere.
Facilities:	Rooms: General: P

PETERBOROUGH

Graham Guesthouse ♦♦♦Guest Accommodation

296 Oundle Road, Peterborough, PE2 9QA

T: +44 (0) 1733 567824
W: tiscover.co.uk/gb/guide/5gb,en/objectId,ACC15394gb/home.html

Bedrooms: 4

Prices: £40.00 per twin room per night, room only

Open: Year round

Description: Friendly and comfortable family-run guesthouse, close to the city centre, ferry meadows and East of England Showground.

Facilities: Rooms:
General: P

SAWTRY

A1 B&B ★★Guest Accommodation

5 High Street, Sawtry, PE28 5SR

T: +44 (0) 1487 830201
E: pat.john@a1bedandbreakfast.co.uk
W: a1bedandbreakfast.co.uk

Bedrooms: 4

Prices: £46.00-£50.00 per twin room per night, room only

Open: Year round

Description: Victorian property overlooking village green. Parking. Central heating. TV in some rooms. Full English breakfast or special needs by request.

Facilities: Rooms:
General: P

PLYMOUTH

Athenaeum Lodge ♦♦♦♦Guest Accommodation

4 Athenaeum Street, The Hoe, Plymouth, PL1 2RQ

T: +44 (0) 1752 665005
E: us@athenaeumlodge.com
W: athenaeumlodge.com

Bedrooms: 10

Prices: £34.00-£50.00 per double room per night, breakfast included
Debit/credit card, cheques/cash accepted

Open: Year round except Christmas and New Year

Description: A family-run Grade II Listed guesthouse close to the Hoe, seafront and leisure pavilions. Recommended by the prestigious *Which?* hotel guide.

Facilities: Rooms:
General: P

PLYMOUTH

Berkeleys of St James ★★★★Guest Accommodation

4 St James Place East, Plymouth, PL1 3AS

T:	+44 (0) 1752 221654
E:	berkeleysofstjames@hotmail.com
W:	smoothhound.co.uk/hotels/berkely2html.
Bedrooms:	5
Prices:	£45.00-£60.00 per double room per night, breakfast included Debit/credit card, cheques/cash accepted
Open:	Year round except Christmas and New Year
Description:	Non-smoking Victorian townhouse ideally situated for seafront, Barbican, theatre, ferry port and city centre. Flexible accommodation between double/twin/triple.
Facilities:	Rooms: General: P

PLYMOUTH

Brittany Guesthouse ★★★Guesthouse

28 Athenaeum Street, The Hoe, Plymouth, PL1 2RQ

T:	+44 (0) 1752 262247
E:	jacjchamberlain@btinternet.com
W:	brittanyguesthouse.co.uk
Bedrooms:	18
Prices:	£38.00-£49.00 per double room per night, breakfast included Debit/credit card, cheques/cash accepted
Open:	Year round except Christmas and New Year
Description:	Close shops, sea front, en suite full English/vegetarian breakfast available, car park.
Facilities:	Rooms: General: P

PLYMOUTH

Caledonia Guesthouse ★★★★Guesthouse

27 Athenaeum Street, Plymouth, PL1 2RQ

T:	+44 (0) 1752 229052
E:	info@thecaledonia.co.uk
W:	thecaledonia.co.uk
Bedrooms:	9
Prices:	£35.00-£50.00 per double room per night, breakfast included Debit/credit card accepted
Open:	Year round except Christmas and New Year
Description:	Welcome to our Victorian guesthouse on Plymouth Hoe, where we are central to all of Plymouth's attractions.
Facilities:	Rooms: General: P

PLYMOUTH

Casa Mia Guesthouse ★★★Guesthouse

201 Citadel Road East, The Hoe, Plymouth, PL1 2JF

T:	+44 (0) 1752 265742
E:	fletcher@cons10.freeserve.co.uk
W:	casa-mia-onthehoe.com
Bedrooms:	7
Prices:	£45.00-£60.00 per double room per night, room only
Open:	Seasonal opening – contact for details
Description:	The location of Casa Mia could not be more convenient as it is placed equally between The Hoe, City Centre and the Barbican. There are many restaurants, pubs, and cafes a short walk away and a continental lifestyle flourishes.
Facilities:	Rooms: General: **P**

PLYMOUTH

Crescent House Hotel ♦♦♦Guest Accommodation

18 Garden Crescent, West Hoe, Plymouth, PL1 3DA

T:	+44 (0) 1752 266424
Bedrooms:	7
Prices:	£36.00-£40.00 per double room per night, breakfast included Cheques/cash, euros accepted
Open:	Seasonal opening – contact for details
Description:	Close to the seafront, city centre and Britanny Ferry terminal. A family-run, friendly hotel with a generous English or continental breakfast on waking.
Facilities:	Rooms: General: **P** Leisure:

PLYMOUTH

Four Seasons ★★★★Guesthouse

207 Citadel Road East, Plymouth, PL1 2JF

T:	+44 (0) 1752 223591
W:	fourseasonsguesthouse.co.uk
Bedrooms:	7
Prices:	£45.00-£55.00 per double room per night, breakfast included Debit/credit card, cheques/cash, euros accepted
Open:	Year round except Christmas and New Year
Description:	This well presented property is located close to the seafront, Hoe and city centre. It has a friendly and relaxed atmosphere. Bedrooms are light and airy mostly with own shower/WC facilities. Colour TV and tea-/coffee-making facilities in rooms.
Facilities:	Rooms: General:

PLYMOUTH

Gabber Farm

★★★Farmhouse

Gabber Lane, Down Thomas, Plymouth, PL9 0AW

T: +44 (0) 1752 862269
E: gabberfarm@tiscali.co.uk

Bedrooms: 5

Prices: £44.00-£50.00 per double room per night, breakfast included
Debit/credit card, cheques/cash, euros accepted

Open: Year round

Description: Directions are provided to farm, on the south Devon coast near Bovisand and Wembury. Good food and friendly welcome assured. Lovely walks in surrounding district, also near Mount Batten centre.

Facilities: Rooms:
General:

PLYMOUTH

Hotspur Guesthouse

★★★Guesthouse

108 North Road East, Plymouth, PL4 6AW

T: +44 (0) 1752 663928
E: info@hotspurguesthouse.co.uk
W: hotspurguesthouse.co.uk

Bedrooms: 10

Prices: £45.00-£48.00 per double room per night, breakfast included
Debit/credit card accepted

Open: Year round

Description: The Hotspur is a traditional guesthouse situated in an ideal position near the city centre, railway and bus station.

Facilities: Rooms:
General:
Leisure:

PLYMOUTH

Mariners Guesthouse

★★★Guesthouse

11 Pier Street, West Hoe, Plymouth, PL1 3BS

T: +44 (0) 1752 261778
E: marinersguesthouse@blueyonder.co.uk
W: marinersguesthouse.co.uk

Bedrooms: 8

Prices: £38.00-£44.00 per double room per night, breakfast included
Debit/credit card accepted

Open: Seasonal opening – contact for details

Description: A warm welcome is guaranteed at our attractive period guesthouse adjacent to Plymouth Hoe and all main tourist attractions.

Facilities: Rooms:
General:

PLYMOUTH

Old Pier Guesthouse

★★★Guesthouse

20 Radford Road, Plymouth, PL1 3BY

T: +44 (0) 1752 268468
E: enquiries@oldpier.co.uk
W: oldpier.co.uk

Bedrooms: 6

Prices: £40.00-£60.00 per double room per night, breakfast included
Debit/credit card, euros accepted

Open: Year round except Christmas and New Year

Description: Plymouth seafront 100m. Walking distance city centre, theatre, Barbican, Brittany Ferries, smoking lounge. Walkers, cyclists, special diets welcome.

Facilities: Rooms:
General:

PLYMOUTH

Osmond Guesthouse

★★★★Guesthouse

42 Pier Street, Plymouth, PL1 3BT

T: +44 (0) 1752 229705
E: info@osmondguesthouse.co.uk
W: osmondguesthouse.co.uk

Bedrooms: 6

Prices: £38.00-£50.00 per double room per night, breakfast included
Debit/credit card, cheques/cash accepted

Open: Year round

Description: Edwardian house 20 yards from seafront. Walking distance to all of Plymouth's points of interest. Courtesy pick up service from stations. Non-smoking house.

Facilities: Rooms:
General: P

PLYMOUTH

Poppy's Guesthouse

♦♦♦Guest Accommodation

4 Alfred Street, The Hoe, Plymouth, PL1 2RP

T: +44 (0) 1752 670452
W: poppysguesthouse.co.uk

Bedrooms: 7

Prices: £36.00-£46.00 per double room per night, breakfast included
Debit/credit card, cheques/cash accepted

Open: Seasonal opening – contact for details

Description: Poppy's is a small, family-run business with friendly hosts and very good standards all round.

Facilities: Rooms:
General: P

PLYMOUTH

Rosaland Hotel

♦♦♦♦Guest Accommodation

32 Houndiscombe Road, Plymouth, PL4 6HQ

T:	+44 (0) 1752 664749
E:	manager@rosalandhotel.com
W:	rosalandhotel.com
Bedrooms:	9
Prices:	£38.00-£50.00 per double room per night, breakfast included Debit/credit card accepted
Open:	Year round
Description:	Fully modernised and refurbished. Close to shops, station, and university, and within walking distance of Hoe and Barbican. Resident owners.
Facilities:	Rooms: General: P

PLYMOUTH

Seymour Guesthouse

★★Guesthouse

211 Citadel Road East, The Hoe, Plymouth, PL1 2JF

T:	+44 (0) 1752 667002
E:	peter@seymourguesthouse.co.uk
Bedrooms:	8
Prices:	£36.00-£44.00 per double room per night, breakfast included Debit/credit card, cheques/cash accepted
Open:	Year round
Description:	A small, family-run guesthouse located opposite Hoe Park and convenient to Barbican, city centre, ferry port and university.
Facilities:	Rooms: General:

PLYMOUTH

Squires Guesthouse

♦♦♦♦Guest Accommodation

7 St James Place East, Plymouth, PL1 3AS

T:	+44 (0) 1752 261459
E:	squiresguesthouse@yahoo.co.uk
W:	squiresguesthouse.20m.com
Bedrooms:	7
Prices:	£45.00-£50.00 per double room per night, breakfast included Debit/credit card, cheques/cash accepted
Open:	Year round
Description:	Elegant Victorian guesthouse in a quiet, secluded square on Plymouth Hoe converted to a very high standard. Within easy walking distance of all amenities.
Facilities:	Rooms: General: P

PLYMOUTH

Sydney Guesthouse

♦♦Guest Accommodation

181 North Road West, Plymouth, PL1 5DE

T:	+44 (0) 1752 266541
Bedrooms:	10
Prices:	£32.00-£48.00 per double room per night, breakfast included
Open:	Year round except Christmas and New Year
Description:	Walking distance of city centre, railway station, university and ferry port.
Facilities:	Rooms: General:

PLYMOUTH

The Cranbourne

★★★Guesthouse

278-282 Citadel Road, Plymouth, PL1 2PZ

T: **E:** **W:**	+44 (0) 1752 263858 cran.hotel@virgin.net cranbournehotel.co.uk
Bedrooms:	40
Prices:	£40.00-£55.00 per double room per night, breakfast included Debit/credit card, cheques/cash, euros accepted
Open:	Year round
Description:	Family-run hotel 200 yards from Plymouth Hoe. Ideal for Brittany Ferries, Hoe, Theatre Royal, Pavilions and city centre. Large car park (secure).
Facilities:	Rooms: General:

PLYMOUTH

The Moorings Guesthouse

★★★Guest Accommodation

4 Garden Crescent, West Hoe, Plymouth, PL1 3DA

T: **E:** **W:**	+44 (0) 1752 250128 enquiries@themooringsguesthouseplymouth.com themooringsguesthouseplymouth.com
Bedrooms:	8
Prices:	£36.00-£45.00 per double room per night, breakfast included Debit/credit card, euros accepted
Open:	Seasonal opening – contact for details
Description:	Warm and friendly family-run guesthouse with extremely high standards. Close to the city centre, Hoe and historic Barbican.
Facilities:	Rooms: General:

PLYMOUTH

Tudor House ★★★Guest Accommodation

105 Citadel Road, The Hoe, Plymouth, PL1 2RN

T:	+44 (0) 1752 661557
W:	smoothhound.co.uk/hotels/tudor-house
Bedrooms:	8
Prices:	£38.00-£45.00 per double room per night, breakfast included Debit/credit card accepted
Open:	Seasonal opening – contact for details
Description:	Centrally situated for sea-front, city centre and ferry terminal. Offering accommodation at reasonable prices.
Facilities:	Rooms: General: P

PLYMOUTH

Westwinds Guesthouse ★★★Guest Accommodation

99 Citadel Road, The Hoe, Plymouth, PL1 2RN

T:	+44 (0) 1752 601777
E:	enquiries@westwindsplymouth.co.uk
W:	westwindsplymouth.co.uk
Bedrooms:	9
Prices:	£40.00-£50.00 per double room per night, breakfast included Debit/credit card, cheques/cash accepted
Open:	Year round except Christmas
Description:	A family-owned B&B which takes pride in looking after its guests in a professional, friendly and homely environment.
Facilities:	Rooms: General: P

SALTASH

Haye Farm ♦♦♦♦Guest Accommodation

Landulph, Saltash, PL12 6QQ

T:	+44 (0) 1752 842786
W:	hayefarmcornwall.co.uk
Bedrooms:	3
Prices:	£45.00-£50.00 per double room per night, breakfast included
Open:	Year round
Description:	Relax in the tranquil setting and enjoy the freedom of the countryside in an Area of Outstanding Natural Beauty. Haye Farm is on the banks of the River Tamar, 25 minutes from the maritime city of Plymouth.
Facilities:	Leisure:

SALTASH

Kilna House
★★Guest Accommodation

Tideford, Saltash, PL12 5AD

T:	+44 (0) 1752 851236
E:	kilnahouse01@aol.com
W:	kilnaguesthouse.co.uk
Bedrooms:	4
Prices:	£48.00 per double room per night, breakfast included
Open:	Year round
Description:	Detached country house. Parts of which date back to 17thC. Overlooking the beautiful Tiddy Valley. All rooms have pleasant country views of rolling pasture land. Dogs are especially welcome as it has two acres of informal gardens.
Facilities:	Rooms: General:

TORPOINT

Stone Farm
♦♦♦♦Guest Accommodation

Whitsand Bay, Millbrook, Torpoint, PL10 1JJ — SILVER AWARD

T:	+44 (0) 1752 822267
E:	blake@stone-farm.fsnet.co.uk
W:	stone-farm.co.uk
Bedrooms:	2
Prices:	£25.00-£28.00 per double room per night, breakfast included Debit/credit card accepted
Open:	Year round
Description:	We offer a high standard of accommodation in an area of outstanding beauty, with a relaxing atmosphere, warm friendly welcome on our working family farm.
Facilities:	Leisure:

YELVERTON

Torrfields
★★★★B&B

Sheepstor, Yelverton, PL20 6PF

T:	+44 (0) 1822 852161
E:	lbsrseabrook@aol.com
W:	torrfieldsbb.co.uk
Bedrooms:	3
Prices:	£40.00 per double room per night, breakfast included Cheques/cash accepted
Open:	Year round except Christmas and New Year
Description:	Detached property in own grounds. Direct access onto moorland. Good views. Super setting. In Dartmoor National Park. Ideal for walkers.
Facilities:	Rooms: TV General: P Leisure:

FAREHAM

Bridge House ★★★★B&B

1 Waterside Gardens, Wallington, Fareham, PO16 8SD

T:	+44 (0) 1329 287775
E:	maryhb8@aol.com
Bedrooms:	2
Prices:	£35.00-£39.00 per twin room per night, breakfast included
Open:	Year round except Christmas and New Year
Description:	Georgian-style family house with Japanese garden. Easy access to the M27 to Southampton, Winchester, Chichester, Portsmouth, the Isle of Wight, cross-channel ferry and airport.
Facilities:	Rooms: General: P

FAREHAM

Trevon Cottage Guesthouse ★★B&B

1 Catisfield Lane, Fareham, PO15 5NW

T:	+44 (0) 1329 843301
Bedrooms:	6
Prices:	£45.00-£60.00 per double room per night, breakfast included Cheques/cash accepted
Open:	Year round except Christmas and New Year
Description:	Period Georgian house, c1735, close to open countryside, four miles from sea. Off A27 in Catisfield village near Titchfield.
Facilities:	Rooms: TV General: P

FAREHAM

Seven Sevens Guesthouse ♦♦♦Guest Accommodation

56 Hill Head Road, Fareham, PO14 3JL

T:	+44 (0) 1329 662408
Bedrooms:	5
Prices:	£45.00-£50.00 per double room per night, breakfast included
Open:	Year round Closed New Year
Description:	Unusual design, B&B residence overlooking the Solent to the Isle of Wight. Clean and comfortable rooms, with TV, hot and cold water and tea-/coffee-making facilities. Off-road parking and close to the beach.
Facilities:	Rooms: TV General: P

FAREHAM

Solent View
♦♦♦Guest Accommodation

361 Warsash Road, Titchfield Common, Fareham, PO14 4LL

T:	+44 (0) 1489 582666
E:	info@solentview.co.uk
W:	solentview.co.uk
Bedrooms:	2
Prices:	£35.00-£60.00 per double room per night, breakfast included
Open:	Year round except Christmas and New Year
Description:	At Solent View we pride ourselves on our hospitality so along with fabulous rooms we also provide exceptionally good breakfasts!
Facilities:	Rooms: General: P

GOSPORT

Ellachie Guesthouse
★★★★B&B

1 Ellachie Road, Alverstoke, Gosport, PO12 2DP

T:	+44 (0) 23 586258
E:	info@ellachie.co.uk
W:	ellachie.co.uk
Bedrooms:	2
Prices:	£45.00 per double room per night, breakfast included
Open:	Year round
Description:	Ellachie Guesthouse is a small family-run business located close to Stokes Bay and the town of Gosport. Portsmouth, Fareham and Southampton are all within easy reach.
Facilities:	Call for details

GOSPORT

Spring Garden Guesthouse
♦♦Guest Accommodation

Spring Garden Lane, Gosport, PO12 1LP

T:	+44 (0) 23 9251 0336
E:	mike.york1@ntlworld.com
Bedrooms:	10
Prices:	£40.00-£50.00 per double room per night, breakfast included Cheques/cash accepted
Open:	Year round except Christmas and New Year
Description:	Large Victorian house run as a warm and friendly licensed guesthouse. Close to town centre and ferries to Portsmouth and Isle of Wight.
Facilities:	Rooms: General: P Leisure:

HAYLING ISLAND

Maidlings

★★★B&B

55 Staunton Avenue, Hayling Island, PO11 0EW

T:	+44 (0) 23 9246 6357
Bedrooms:	3
Prices:	£48.00-£52.00 per double room per night, breakfast included
Open:	Year round except Christmas
Description:	Quality accommodation in detached home, close to the beach, golf course, sailing and Hayling Billy coastal path.
Facilities:	Rooms: General: **P**

LEE-ON-SOLENT

Chester Lodge

★★★★B&B

20 Chester Crescent, Lee-on-the-Solent, PO13 9BH

T: **E:**	+44 (0) 23 9255 0894 chesterlodge@btinternet.com
Bedrooms:	3
Prices:	£47.00-£52.00 per double room per night, breakfast included Cheques/cash accepted
Open:	Year round except Christmas and New Year
Description:	The lodge is set in a quiet location, convenient for historical naval attractions, Solent cruises, sailing and beaches.
Facilities:	Rooms: General: **P**

PORTSMOUTH

Leeward House B&B

♦♦♦♦Guest Accommodation

18 Russell Road, Lee-on-the-Solent, PO13 9HP

T: **E:** **W:**	+44 (0) 23 9255 6090 enq@leewardhouse.co.uk leewardhouse.co.uk
Bedrooms:	3
Prices:	£40.00-£50.00 per double room per night, breakfast included
Open:	Year round except Christmas
Description:	Comfortable accommodation in quiet road close to beach. Easy access to M27 and M3, making Lee-on-Solent the perfect location for business or pleasure.
Facilities:	Rooms: General: **P**

PORTSMOUTH

Everley Guesthouse ★★★Guest Accommodation

33 Festing Road, Southsea, Portsmouth, PO4 0NG

T:	+44 (0) 23 9273 1001
E:	everleyguesthouse@ntlworld.com
Bedrooms:	9
Prices:	£46.00 per double room per night, breakfast included Debit/credit card accepted
Open:	Seasonal opening
Description:	Everley is bright and cheerfully decorated with good food, friendly atmosphere and en suite rooms. Ownership changed in July 2003.
Facilities:	Rooms: General:

RYDE

Burchfield ★★★B&B

1 Dover Street, Ryde, PO33 2AQ

T:	+44 (0) 1983 568880
E:	burchfieldbedandbreakfast@hotmail.com
Bedrooms:	2
Prices:	£45.00 per double room per night, breakfast included
Open:	Seasonal opening – contact for details
Description:	Burchfield B&B is situated opposite the Esplanade, the harbour and the beach. Shops, restaurants, bars, cafes and nightclubs are all within walking distance.
Facilities:	Rooms:

RYDE

Dorset Hotel ★★★Guest Accommodation

31 Dover Street, Ryde, PO33 2BW

T:	+44 (0) 1983 564327
E:	hoteldorset@aol.com
W:	thedorsethotel.co.uk
Bedrooms:	23
Prices:	£47.00 per double room per night, breakfast included Debit/credit card, euros accepted
Open:	Seasonal opening – contact for details
Description:	Pleasantly situated two-three minutes from Ryde's six miles of sandy beaches and famous esplanade. Excellent shopping and a range of bars and restaurants are nearby, as are the rail, boat, hovercraft, bus and coach terminals.
Facilities:	Rooms: General: Leisure:

RYDE

Sea View ★★★B&B

8 Dover Street, Ryde, PO33 2AQ

T: +44 (0) 1983 810976
E: seaviewbandbinryde@hotmail.com

Bedrooms: 2

Prices: £40.00 per double room per night, breakfast included

Open: Seasonal opening – contact for details

Description: There is a warm welcome for all guests at this comfortable, non-smoking B&B. Open all winter, except Christmas and New Year.

Facilities: Rooms:

SOUTHSEA

Esk Vale Guesthouse ♦♦♦Guest Accommodation

39 Granada Road, Southsea, PO4 0Road

T: +44 (0) 23 9286 2639
E: enquires@eskvaleguesthouse.co.uk
W: eskvaleguesthouse.co.uk

Bedrooms: 6

Prices: £40.00-£48.00 per double room per night, breakfast included
Cheques/cash, euros accepted

Open: Year round except Christmas and New Year

Description: Victorian house with all modern facilities including car parking. All rooms en suite with two family rooms.

Facilities: Rooms:
General: P

SOUTHSEA

Gainsborough House ♦♦♦Guest Accommodation

9 Malvern Road, Southsea, PO5 2LZ

T: +44 (0) 23 9282 2604

Bedrooms: 7

Prices: £42.00 per double room per night, breakfast included

Open: Year round except Christmas and New Year

Description: A long-established guesthouse, just off the seafront, opposite the Pyramids.

Facilities: Rooms:
General:

SOUTHSEA

Homestead Guesthouse ♦♦♦Guest Accommodation

11 Bembridge Crescent, Southsea, PO4 0QT

T: +44 (0) 23 9273 2362
E: b.currie1@ntlworld.com
W: steadguesthouse-southsea.co.uk

Bedrooms: 6

Prices: £44.00-£48.00 per double room per night, breakfast included

Open: Year round except Christmas and New Year

Description: Family-run guesthouse, close to beach and pier. Tea/coffee-making facilities and colour TVs are available in all bedrooms. Children very welcome.

Facilities: Rooms:
General:

SOUTHSEA

Portsmouth & Southsea Backpackers Lodge ★Hostel

4 Florence Road, Southsea, PO5 2NE

T: +44 (0) 23 9283 2495
E: portsmouthbackpackers@hotmail.com
W: portsmouthbackpackers.co.uk

Bedrooms: 19

Prices: £26.00-£29.00 per person per night, room only
Cheques/cash accepted

Open: Year round

Description: Family-run, independent hostel for self-catering travellers, centrally situated for all attractions. Large social areas indoors/outdoors. Secure cycle storage.

Facilities: Rooms:
General: P
Leisure:

SOUTHSEA

Victoria Court ★★★Guest Accommodation

29 Victoria Road North, Southsea, PO5 1PL

T: +44 (0) 23 9282 0305
E: stay@victoriacourt.co.uk
W: victoriacourt.co.uk

Bedrooms: 5

Prices: £40.00-£55.00 per double room per night, breakfast included
Debit/credit card, euros accepted

Open: Year round Closed New Year

Description: Set in the heart of Southsea, offering a secluded dining room depicting family association with Portsmouth and naval heritage.

Facilities: Rooms:
General:
Leisure:

SOUTHSEA

Woodville Hotel ♦♦♦Guest Accommodation

6 Florence Road, Southsea, PO5 2NE

T: +44 (0) 23 9282 3409
E: woodvillehotel@boltblue.com

Bedrooms: 10

Prices: £42.00-£55.00 per double room per night, breakfast included
Debit/credit card, cheques/cash accepted

Open: Year round except Christmas and New Year

Description: Family-run hotel, two minutes from the sea and central for all Southsea's amenities. Large car park in grounds.
Fully licensed.

Facilities: Rooms:
General: P

WATERLOOVILLE

Ashdown ♦♦♦♦Guest Accommodation

33 Ferndale, Waterlooville, PO7 7PH

T: +44 (0) 23 9226 2607
E: ashdown.jennyancill@btopenworld.com

Bedrooms: 1

Prices: £35.00-£60.00 per double room per night, breakfast included

Open: Year round except Christmas and New Year

Description: Ashdown is a detached home, attractively furnished and set in a quiet residential location. French doors in the dining room open out onto the terrace and large, pretty garden.

Facilities: Rooms:
General:

WATERLOOVILLE

Cams ♦♦♦Guest Accommodation

Cams Hill Lane, Hambledon, Waterlooville, PO7 4SP

T: +44 (0) 23 9263 2865

Bedrooms: 4

Prices: £48.00-£56.00 per double room per night, breakfast included

Open: Year round except Christmas and New Year

Description: A 17thC Listed farmhouse in beautiful setting with large garden, paddocks and tennis court. On edge of Hambledon village. Excellent centre for sightseeing and walking.
Just off B2150.

Facilities: Rooms:
General: P
Leisure:

WATERLOOVILLE

Holly Dale ♦♦♦♦Guest Accommodation

11 Lovedean Lane, Waterlooville, PO8 8HH

T: +44 (0) 23 9259 2047
E: pwengland@uku.co.uk

Bedrooms: 3

Prices: £42.00-£45.00 per twin room per night, breakfast included

Open: Year round except Christmas and New Year

Description: Friendly, family-run B&B with large garden. Twin en suite and two single rooms available, all with TV and tea-/coffee-making facilities. Portsmouth and countryside within easy reach.

Facilities: Rooms:
General:

WATERLOOVILLE

New Haven B&B ★★★B&B

193 London Road, Waterlooville, PO7 7RN

T: +44 (0) 23 9226 8559

Bedrooms: 4

Prices: £40.00-£50.00 per double room per night, breakfast included
Cheques/cash accepted

Open: Year round

Description: A warm welcome awaits you in our spacious home. We offer you comfortably equipped en suite rooms with full English and continental breakfast.

Facilities: Rooms:
General:

WATERLOOVILLE

The Ship & Bell Hotel ♦♦♦Guest Accommodation

6 London Road, Horndean, Waterlooville, PO8 0BZ

T: +44 (0) 23 9259 2107
E: shipandbell@accommodating-inns.co.uk
W: accommodating-inns.co.uk

Bedrooms: 14

Prices: £42.00 per double room per night, breakfast included
Debit/credit card accepted

Open: Year round

Description: A former 17thC coaching inn with plenty of character. Now a family-run hotel and bar just off the A3(M), next to the George Gale brewery.

Facilities: Rooms:
General:
Leisure:

CHESTERFIELD

Abigail's Guesthouse ♦♦♦Guest Accommodation

62 Brockwell Lane, Chesterfield, S40 4EE

T: +44 (0) 1246 279391
E: gail@abigails.fsnet.co.uk
W: abigailsguesthouse.co.uk

Bedrooms: 7

Prices: £46.00 per double room per night, breakfast included

Open: Year round

Description: Relax while eating breakfast in the conservatory overlooking panoramic views of Chesterfield and the surrounding moorlands. Winner of the Heart of England Tourist Board's Best B&B 2000.

Facilities: Rooms:
General: **P**

CHESTERFIELD

Maylands Guesthouse ★★★Guesthouse

56 Sheffield Road, Chesterfield, S41 7LS

T: +44 (0) 1246 233602

Bedrooms: 5

Prices: £23.00-£44.00 per double room per night, breakfast included

Open: Year round

Description: A lovely, homely detached house with beautiful garden and car park. All rooms traditionally furnished with hospitality tray and Sky TV. Full fire certificate. Lovely Victorian four-poster bedroom. A good and plentiful English breakfast.

Facilities: Rooms: TV
General: **P**

CHESTERFIELD

Stone Croft ★★★★B&B

15 Church Street, Barlborough, Chesterfield, S43 4ER

T: +44 (0) 1246 810974
E: june@stone-croft.co.uk
W: stone-croft.co.uk

Bedrooms: 1

Prices: £42.00 per double room per night, breakfast included

Open: Year round

Description: Stone Croft is a Grade II Listed building set in 2/3 of an acre garden. Homely with plenty of room for parking. Barlborough is an ideal base for touring the area's attractions. Just off the M1 jct 30 and close to Sheffield.

Facilities: Rooms:
General: **P**

DRONFIELD

Carpenter House

★★★★B&B

Cordwell Lane, Millthorpe, Dronfield, S18 7WH

T:	+44 (0) 114 289 0307
Bedrooms:	2
Prices:	£30.00-£45.00 per double room per night, breakfast included
Open:	Year round
Description:	A beautiful country house with local cricket club within its grounds. Close to Sheffield, Chesterfield, the Peak District and Chatsworth. It is ideal for tourists and has all the facilities you expect in this four star accommodation.
Facilities:	Rooms: General: **P**

SHEFFIELD

Cassita

♦♦♦♦Guest Accommodation

off Snape Hill Lane, Dronfield, S18 2GL

T:	+44 (0) 1246 417303
Bedrooms:	1
Prices:	£27.00-£45.00 per twin room per night, breakfast included
Open:	Year round
Description:	In Dronfield centre yet in a quiet, private location. We offer visitors a warm welcome and comfortable accommodation in a ground floor annexe, with own entrance, overlooking mature garden. Local amenities within walking distance.
Facilities:	Rooms: General: **P**

DRONFIELD

Cordwell House

★★★★B&B

Cordwell Lane, Millthorpe, Dronfield, S18 7WH

T:	+44 (0) 114 289 0271
Bedrooms:	4
Prices:	£30.00-£60.00 per double room per night, breakfast included
Open:	Year round
Description:	Delightful stone-built cottage dating to the 17thC, is in the beautiful Cordwell Valley, on the edge of the Peak National Park yet only 20 minutes from Chesterfield and Sheffield. Bedrooms are of the highest standard.
Facilities:	Rooms: General: **P**

DRONFIELD

Woodview Cottage ★★★★B&B

Millcross Lane, Barlow, Dronfield, S18 7TA

T: +44 (0) 114 289 0724
E: ter.crisbarnard@btopenworld.com
W: woodviewcottage.co.uk

Bedrooms: 3

Prices: £28.00-£42.00 per double room per night, breakfast included

Open: Year round

Description: Woodview Cottage is in a quiet, country village surrounded by fields and woods with many picturesque walks. Comfortably furnished with attention to detail to make your stay as relaxing and enjoyable as possible. Local inns serve good food.

Facilities: General: [symbols]
Leisure: [symbols]

HOPE VALLEY

YHA Hathersage ★★Hostel

The Hollies, Castleton Road, Hope Valley, S32 1EH

T: +44 (0) 870 770 5852
W: yha.org.uk

Bedrooms: 9

Prices: £8.00-£11.00 per person per night, breakfast included
Debit/credit card accepted

Open: Year round

Description: A large Victorian house on the edge of Hathersage village in the Peak National Park. On the cusp of the white and dark peak, it is the ideal centre for climbers, walkers and cyclists of all levels.

Facilities: Rooms: [symbols]
General: [symbols]

ROTHERHAM

Fitzwilliam Arms Hotel ♦♦♦Guest Accommodation

Taylors Lane, Parkgate, Rotherham, S62 6EE

T: +44 (0) 1709 522744
E: ronhull@ronhull.freeserve.co.uk

Bedrooms: 18

Prices: £35.00-£43.50 per double room per night, breakfast included
Debit/credit card accepted

Open: Year round

Description: Fitzwilliam Arms Hotel is an inn with a friendly atmosphere close to Magna Visitor Centre and Meadowhall Shopping Complex. Within easy reach of Sheffield Arena, Don Valley Stadium and Ice Sheffield.

Facilities: Rooms: [symbols]
General: [symbols]
Leisure: [symbols]

SHEFFIELD

Beighton B&B

♦♦♦Guest Accommodation

48-50 High Street, Beighton, Sheffield, S20 1EA

T:	+44 (0) 114 269 2004
E:	Beightonbandb@aol.com
W:	Beightonbandb.co.uk
Bedrooms:	9
Prices:	£40.00-£45.00 per double room per night, breakfast included
Open:	Year round
Description:	Beighton B&B is within easy reach of Meadowhall Arena, Don Valley Stadium, Rother Valley Country Park, Crystal Peak Shopping Complex and 40 minutes from Chatsworth House.
Facilities:	Rooms: General: P

SHEFFIELD

Coniston Guesthouse

♦♦♦Guest Accommodation

90 Beechwood Road, Hillsborough, Sheffield, S6 4LQ

T:	+44 (0) 114 233 9680
E:	conistonguest@freeuk.com
W:	conistonguest@freeuk.com
Bedrooms:	6
Prices:	£46.00 per double room per night, breakfast included
Open:	Year round
Description:	Detached Victorian house. Approximately 2.5 miles to the city centre. Only five minutes from the countryside and three miles from Sheffield Arena.
Facilities:	Rooms: General: P

SHEFFIELD

Gulliver's B&B

★★★Guest Accommodation

167 Ecclesall Road South, Sheffield, S11 9PN

T:	+44 (0) 114 262 0729
Bedrooms:	3
Prices:	£43.00 per double room per night, breakfast included
Open:	Seasonal opening Closed New Year
Description:	Attractive Victorian house situated in top residential area close to city centre, university and on the outskirts of the Peak District.
Facilities:	Rooms: General: P

SHEFFIELD

Ivory House Hotel ★★★Guest Accommodation

34 Wostenholm Road, Sheffield, S7 1LJ

T: +44 (0) 114 255 1853
E: ivoryhousehotel@amserve.com

Bedrooms: 8

Prices: £40.00-£46.00 per double room per night, breakfast included
Debit/credit card accepted

Open: Seasonal opening – contact for details

Description: Ivory House is a small, family-run hotel, only one mile south west of Sheffield city. Built in 1860, this grand detached Victorian property offers a good selection of comfortable accommodation from single en suite to large family room.

Facilities: Rooms:
General: P

SHEFFIELD

Riverside Court Hotel ♦♦Guest Accommodation

4 Nursery Street, Sheffield, S3 8GG

T: +44 (0) 114 273 1962
E: enquire@riversidecourt.co.uk
W: riversidecourt.co.uk

Bedrooms: 35

Prices: £47.00-£59.00 per double room per night, room only

Open: Seasonal opening – contact for details

Description: A city centre, family-run hotel, all 35 rooms offer en suite facilities. Residents-only bar, satellite TV. Self-catering facilities also available. Private car parking.

Facilities: Rooms:
General: P
Leisure:

SHEFFIELD

The Noose and Gibbet ★Inn

97 Broughton Lane, Attercliffe, Sheffield, S9 2DE

T: +44 (0) 114 261 7182
E: please@call.above.number.uk

Bedrooms: 12

Prices: £40.00 per double room per night, room only

Open: Year round

Description: An 18thC pub and B&B. Themed on Spence Broughton, the local villain and highwayman.

Facilities: Rooms:
General:

SHEFFIELD

Tyndale
♦♦♦Guest Accommodation

164 Millhouses Lane, Sheffield, S7 2HE

T:	+44 (0) 114 236 1660
Bedrooms:	3
Prices:	£44.00-£46.00 per double room per night, breakfast included
Open:	Year round
Description:	Comfortable, family home with emphasis on food and a friendly atmosphere. Three miles from the city centre and the Peak District.
Facilities:	Rooms: General: **P**

CONGLETON

The Woodlands
♦♦♦♦Guest Accommodation

Quarry Wood Farm, Wood Street, Congleton, CW12 1AH

T:	+44 (0) 1782 518877
Bedrooms:	3
Prices:	£40.00-£55.00 per double room per night, breakfast included
Open:	Seasonal opening – contact for details
Description:	Large modern farmhouse set in 90 acres of woodland and farmland. Fantastic views, outdoor swimming pool with changing facilities. Large garden for guests.
Facilities:	Rooms: TV CDP General: **P** Leisure:

LEEK

Brook House Farm
♦♦♦Guest Accommodation

Brookhouse Farm, Brookhouse Lane, Leek, ST13 7DF

T:	+44 (0) 1538 360296
Bedrooms:	5
Prices:	£40.00-£50.00 per double room per night, breakfast included
Open:	Year round
Description:	A stock rearing farm in a peaceful valley. Ideal for visiting Peak District, Potteries, Alton Towers, Churnet Valley Steam Railway, Caudon Canal and Coombes Valley RSPB reserve.
Facilities:	General: **P**

LEEK

Middle Farm

★★★Guest Accommodation

Middle Farm, Apesford, Leek, ST13 7EX

T: +44 (0) 1538 382839
E: susan@middlefarmbandb.co.uk
W: middlefarmbandb.co.uk

Bedrooms: 7

Prices: £48.00 per double room per night, breakfast included

Open: Year round

Description: Just off the main Leek-Ashbourne road this large, renovated farmhouse is set in peaceful countryside. Ideal location from which to explore the Peak District, Potteries and Alton Towers.

Facilities: General: P

LEEK

Mosslee Grange B&B

★★★B&B

Basford Green, Cheddleton, Leek, ST13 7ES

T: +44 (0) 7969 463685

Bedrooms: 6

Prices: £44.00-£50.00 per double room per night, breakfast included
Euros accepted

Open: Year round except Christmas and New Year

Description: Contemporary barn conversion offering B&B accommodation within beautiful area, convenient for Alton Towers, Peak District and Potteries.

Facilities: Rooms:
General: P

NEWCASTLE UNDER LYME

New Hayes Farm

★★★★Farmhouse

Trentham Road, Butterton, Newcastle Under Lyme, ST5 4DX

T: +44 (0) 1782 680889
E: info@newhayesfarm.co.uk
W: newhayesfarm.co.uk

Bedrooms: 3

Prices: £45.00-£70.00 per double room per night, breakfast included

Open: Seasonal opening – closed New Year

Description: A warm welcome awaits at our attractive Victorian farmhouse on a dairy farm. Spacious comfortable en suite bedrooms. Keele University four miles, convenient for Stoke-on-Trent, Trentham, Alton Towers 20 miles. Five minutes to M6 jct 15.

Facilities: Rooms:
General: P

STOKE-ON-TRENT

Chapel Croft B&B ★★★★Guesthouse

Chapel Croft, Newtown Road, Stoke-on-Trent, ST8 7SW

T:	+44 (0) 1782 511013
E:	chapelcroft@biddulphpark.freeserve.co.uk
W:	chapelcroft.com
Bedrooms:	4
Prices:	£38.00 per double room per night, breakfast included
Open:	Year round
Description:	A warm welcome awaits you in our beautiful converted chapel. Quiet location with lovely views and walks. Within easy reach of Biddulph Grange Garden, Potteries, Peak District and Alton Towers.
Facilities:	General: P Leisure:

STOKE-ON-TRENT

Garden Cottage ★★★★B&B

Halls Road, Biddulph, Stoke-on-Trent, ST8 6DB

T:	+44 (0) 1782 510835
E:	hoods@phood9wanadoo.co.uk
Bedrooms:	6
Prices:	£44.00-£58.00 per double room per night, breakfast included Cheques/cash accepted
Open:	Year round except Christmas and New Year
Description:	Welcome to Garden Cottage B&B. Superior rooms, excellent food, walk to Biddulph Grange Gardens, visit the Peak District, Potteries and Alton Towers.
Facilities:	Rooms: TV General: P Leisure:

STOKE-ON-TRENT

Hollinhurst Farm ★★★Farmhouse

Hollinhurst Farm, Park Lane, Stoke-on-Trent, ST9 9JB

T:	+44 (0) 1782 502633
W:	smoothhound.co.uk/hotels/hollinhurst.html
Bedrooms:	3
Prices:	£36.00-£40.00 per double room per night, breakfast included
Open:	Year round
Description:	A stone-built 17thC farmhouse on a working farm which offers the opportunity for tranquil walks in the surrounding countryside.
Facilities:	Rooms: General: P

STOKE-ON-TRENT

Ley Fields Farm ♦♦♦♦Guest Accommodation

Ley Fields Farm, Leek Road, Cheadle,Stoke-on-Trent, ST10 2EF SILVER AWARD

T: +44 (0) 1538 752875
E: leyfieldsfarm@aol.com
W: leyfieldsfarm.co.uk

Bedrooms: 3

Prices: £48.00 per double room per night, breakfast included

Open: Year round

Description: Listed Georgian farmhouse on a stock-rearing farm in beautiful countryside. Luxury bedrooms include a family suite. Recommended in *Which? Good B&B Guide*.

Facilities: General: P

STOKE-ON-TRENT

Moorville Hall Hotel ★★Hotel

Leek Road, Cellarhead, Stoke-on-Trent, ST9 0DG

T: +44 (0) 1782 302326
E: stay@moorvillehall.co.uk
W: moorvillehallhotel.co.uk

Bedrooms: 27

Prices: £48.00 per double room per night, breakfast included

Open: Year round

Description: Located on the outskirts of Stoke-on-Trent, visiting Staffordshire's attractions is easy. Alton Towers, the Peak District, and The Potteries are all 25 minutes away by car. Moorville Hall also has many on-site leisure facilities.

Facilities: Rooms:
General: P
Leisure:

STOKE-ON-TRENT

Northwood Hotel ♦♦♦Guest Accommodation

146 Keelings Road, Northwood, Stoke-on-Trent, ST1 6QA

T: +44 (0) 1782 279729
E: northwoodhotel@city-hotels.org.uk
W: city-hotels.org.uk

Bedrooms: 7

Prices: £42.00 per double room per night, room only

Open: Year round

Description: Located close to the city centre, the hotel offers comfortable accommodation at a competitive rate. Ideally situated for the factory shops, ceramic museums, and city entertainment. Only 20 minutes away from Alton Towers by car.

Facilities: Rooms:
General: P

STOKE-ON-TRENT

Park View Guesthouse
★★★Guesthouse

15 Mill Road, Cheadle, Stoke-on-Trent, ST10 1NG

T: +44 (0) 1538 755412
E: stewart@parkviewguesthouse.fsworld.co.uk
W: theparkviewguesthouse.com

Bedrooms: 8

Prices: £48.00-£75.00 per double room per night, breakfast included
Debit/credit card accepted

Open: Year round except Christmas and New Year

Description: Conveniently situated for Alton Towers, the Potteries and the Peak District. Close to pubs, restaurants and leisure centre. Friendly and welcoming.

Facilities: Rooms:
General: P
Leisure:

STOKE-ON-TRENT

Reynolds Hey Farm
★★★★Guest Accommodation

Reynolds Hey Farm, Park Lane, Stoke-on-Trent, ST9 9JB

T: +44 (0) 1782 502717
E: reynoldshey@hotmail.com
W: reynoldshey.co.uk

Bedrooms: 4

Prices: £44.00 per double room per night, breakfast included

Open: Year round

Description: Set in the rolling countryside, this modernised farmhouse offers comfortable accommodation in a friendly atmosphere. Situated close to The Potteries, Alton Towers, and beautiful Peak District and Caldon Canal.

Facilities: Rooms:
General: P

STOKE-ON-TRENT

Sneyd Arms Hotel
♦♦♦Guest Accommodation

Tower Square, Stoke-on-Trent, ST6 5AA

T: +44 (0) 1782 826722
W: thesneydarms.co.uk

Bedrooms: 14

Prices: £41.00-£50.00 per double room per night, breakfast included
Debit/credit card accepted

Open: Year round

Description: Small, family-run hotel in town centre, restaurant, home cooking our speciality. Public bar and sun beds. En suite and budget accommodation available.

Facilities: Rooms:
General: P
Leisure:

STOKE-ON-TRENT

The Limes B&B ★★★B&B

The Limes, Cheadle Road, Stoke-on-Trent, ST11 9PW

T:	+44 (0) 1782 393278
Bedrooms:	3
Prices:	£23.00 per double room per night, breakfast included
Open:	Year round
Description:	Victorian residence of quality and character, set in large landscaped gardens, with ample parking. The house has a relaxing, welcoming atmosphere with intricate decor and is elegantly furnished. Last arrival time 10pm. No children under five.
Facilities:	Rooms: General: P

STOKE-ON-TRENT

Verdon Guesthouse ★★Guesthouse

44 Charles Street, Stoke-on-Trent, ST1 3JY

T: **E:** **W:**	+44 (0) 1782 264244 debbie@tams6085.fslife.co.uk verdonguesthouse.co.uk
Bedrooms:	13
Prices:	£40.00-£44.00 per double room per night, breakfast included Debit/credit card accepted
Open:	Year round
Description:	Large, friendly guesthouse in Hanley town centre opposite bus station. All rooms have cable TV, tea-/coffee-making facilities. Convenient for Pottery factory visits, Alton Towers.
Facilities:	Rooms: TV General: P

STOKE-ON-TRENT

Victoria Hotel ♦♦♦Guest Accommodation

4 Roundwell Street, Tunstall, Stoke-on-Trent, ST6 5JJ

T: **E:**	+44 (0) 1782 835964 victoria-hotel@tunstall51.fsnet.co.uk
Bedrooms:	9
Prices:	£36.00-£42.00 per double room per night, breakfast included Debit/credit card, cheques/cash,euros accepted
Open:	Year round except Christmas and New Year
Description:	Once a Victorian public house, now a comfortable, family-run guesthouse in a quiet, residential area. City centre is 2.5 miles away, Royal Doulton a mile. Convenient for all Potteries and for Alton Towers (17 miles).
Facilities:	Rooms: TV General: P

BIDFORD-ON-AVON

The Harbour ★★★Guest Accommodation

20 Salford Road, Bidford-on-Avon, B50 4EN

T: +44 (0) 1789 772975
E: peter@theharbour-gh.co.uk
W: theharbour-gh.co.uk

Bedrooms: 6

Prices: £22.50-£25.00 per double room per night, room only

Open: Year round

Description: The Harbour is an attractive black and white period house, built in the 18thC as a farm. It now stands in one acre of well-managed garden. This attractive, tastefully furnished house has three spacious bedrooms.

Facilities: Rooms:
General: **P**
Leisure:

SHIPSTON ON STOUR

Folly Farm Cottage ★★★★Guest Accommodation

Back Street, Ilmington, Shipston on Stour, CV36 4LJ GOLD AWARD

T: +44 (0) 1608 682425
E: sm@follyfarmcottage.co.uk
W: follyfarm.co.uk

Bedrooms: 6

Prices: £26.00-£40.00 per double room per night, room only

Open: Year round

Description: Olde worlde country cottage accommodation. Double or king-size four-poster rooms, en suite bathroom with bath and shower or whirlpool, hospitality tray, clock radio, TV, video, free video library.

Facilities: Rooms:
General: **P**

STRATFORD-UPON-AVON

Aidan Guesthouse ★★★★Guesthouse

11 Evesham Place, Stratford-upon-Avon, CV37 6HT

T: +44 (0) 1789 292824
E: john2aidan@aol.com
W: aidanhouse.co.uk

Bedrooms: 6

Prices: £44.00-£50.00 per double room per night, breakfast included
Debit/credit card, cheques/cash accepted

Open: Year round

Description: Carefully furnished and restored Edwardian townhouse, close theatre and river. Central heating and double glazing throughout. En suite rooms, telephone,tea-/coffee-making facilities and colour TV in each room. Ample parking.

Facilities: Rooms: TV
General: **P**
Leisure:

STRATFORD-UPON-AVON

Arrandale

★★★B&B

208 Evesham Road, Stratford-upon-Avon, CV37 9AS

T: +44 (0) 1789 267112
E: a.mellor5@ntlworld.com
W: arrandale.netfirms.com

Bedrooms: 8

Prices: £17.50-£20.00 per double room per night, room only

Open: Year round

Description: We are a family-run small guesthouse letting double bedrooms at the town end of the B439 Bidford/Evesham Road, 10 minutes' walk from the theatre and Shakespearean properties. The price includes a full English breakfast.

Facilities: Rooms:
General: **P**

STRATFORD-UPON-AVON

Avonlea

★★★★Guesthouse

47 Shipston Road, Stratford-upon-Avon, CV37 7LN

T: +44 (0) 1789 205940
E: avonlea-stratford@lineone.net
W: avonlea-stratford.co.uk

Bedrooms: 7

Prices: £48.00-£78.00 per double room per night, breakfast included
Debit/credit card, cheques/cash, euros accepted

Open: Year round except Christmas

Description: Avonlea is a stylish Victorian townhouse situated only five minutes' walk from the theatre and town centre. All rooms are en suite and furnished to the highest quality.

Facilities: Rooms:
General: **P**

STRATFORD-UPON-AVON

Broadlands Guesthouse

★★★★Guesthouse

23 Evesham Place, Stratford-upon-Avon, CV37 6HT — SILVER AWARD

T: +44 (0) 1789 299181
E: philandjohn@broadlandsguesthouse.co.uk

Bedrooms: 12

Prices: £32.00-£40.00 per double room per night, room only

Open: Year round

Description: Broadlands is a comfortable Victorian-style guesthouse in the Old Town conservation area. Privately owned, Broadlands offers a high standard of accommodation in a relaxed and friendly atmosphere.

Facilities: Rooms:
General: **P**

STRATFORD-UPON-AVON

Carlton Guesthouse ★★★Guesthouse

22 Evesham Place, Stratford-upon-Avon, CV37 6HT

T:	+44 (0) 1789 293548
Bedrooms:	7
Prices:	£20.00-£26.00 per double room per night, breakfast included Cheques/cash accepted
Open:	Year round
Description:	Tasteful decor, elegantly furnished, combining Victorian origins with modern facilities. A peaceful home, happily shared with guests. Private parking.
Facilities:	Rooms: General: **P**

STRATFORD-UPON-AVON

Church Farm ★★★Farmhouse

Dorsington, Stratford-upon-Avon, CV37 8AX

T:	+44 (0) 1789 720471
E:	chfarmdorsington@aol.com
W:	churchfarmstratford.co.uk
Bedrooms:	6
Prices:	£23.00-£27.00 per double room per night, room only
Open:	Year round
Description:	A warm and friendly welcome awaits you at our Georgian farmhouse. Most bedrooms are en suite – all have colour TV and tea-/coffee-making facilities. Some ground floor rooms are in a converted stable block. Central heating in all.
Facilities:	Rooms: General: **P**

STRATFORD-UPON-AVON

Curtain Call Guesthouse ★★★Guesthouse

142 Alcester Road, Stratford-upon-Avon, CV37 9DR

T:	+44 (0) 1789 267734
E:	curtaincall@onetel.com
W:	curtaincallguesthouse.co.uk
Bedrooms:	6
Prices:	£40.00-£70.00 per double room per night, breakfast included Debit/credit card, cheques/cash, euros accepted
Open:	Year round except Christmas
Description:	This cosy guesthouse, situated between the town centre and Anne Hathaway's Cottage will make the ideal base for your stay in Shakespeare Country. All rooms include colour TV, radio alarm clocks and hairdryers.
Facilities:	Rooms: General: **P**

STRATFORD-UPON-AVON

Faviere
★★★★Guest Accommodation

127 Shipston Road, Stratford-upon-Avon, CV37 7LW

T:	+44 (0) 1789 293764
E:	reservations@faviere.com
W:	faviere.com
Bedrooms:	6
Prices:	£40.00-£54.00 per double room per night, breakfast included Cheques/cash accepted
Open:	Year round except Christmas and New Year
Description:	A warm, friendly welcome awaits you at this comfortable family-run guesthouse. It is situated close to the river and a 10 minute walk will take you to the theatre and town centre.
Facilities:	Rooms: General: **P**

STRATFORD-UPON-AVON

Green Gables
★★★B&B

47 Banbury Road, Stratford-upon-Avon, CV37 7HW

T:	+44 (0) 1789 205557
E:	jke985@aol.com
W:	stratford-upon-avon.co.uk/greengables.htm
Bedrooms:	12
Prices:	£20.00-£25.00 per double room per night, room only
Open:	Year round
Description:	We are a comfortable, centrally heated Edwardian house, south of the River Avon, 10 minutes' walk from Stratford Tourist Information Centre and town centre, with parking.
Facilities:	Rooms: General: **P**

STRATFORD-UPON-AVON

Green Haven
★★★★Guesthouse

217 Evesham Road, Stratford-upon-Avon, CV37 9AS

T:	+44 (0) 1789 297874
E:	information@green-haven.co.uk
W:	green-haven.co.uk
Bedrooms:	5
Prices:	£44.00-£52.00 per double room per night, breakfast included Debit/credit card, cheques/cash accepted
Open:	Year round except Christmas
Description:	Situated close to town centre, railway station and Stratford racecourse. All rooms en suite with colour TVs, courtesy trays, private parking and all diets catered for. Non-smoking.
Facilities:	Rooms: General: **P**

STRATFORD-UPON-AVON

Grosvenor Villa

★★★Guesthouse

9 Evesham Place, Stratford-upon-Avon, CV37 6HT

T:	+44 (0) 1789 266192
E:	marion@grosvenorvilla.com
W:	grosvenorvilla.co.uk
Bedrooms:	7
Prices:	£40.00-£52.00 per double room per night, breakfast included Debit/credit card, cheques/cash accepted
Open:	Year round except Christmas
Description:	Grosvenor Villa is an authentically restored Victorian family house 10 minutes' walk from the town centre and theatre.
Facilities:	Rooms: General: P

STRATFORD-UPON-AVON

Heron Lodge

★★★★Guesthouse

260 Alcester Road, Stratford-upon-Avon, CV37 9JQ

T:	+44 (0) 1789 299169
E:	chrisandbob@heronlodge.com
W:	heronlodge.com
Bedrooms:	4
Prices:	£40.00-£56.00 per double room per night, breakfast included Debit/credit card, cheques/cash accepted
Open:	Year round except Christmas and New Year
Description:	Friendly B&B within walking distance of Anne Hathaway's cottage. Private parking, pretty garden and "Inspired Breakfast" award.
Facilities:	Rooms: General: P

STRATFORD-UPON-AVON

Ingon Bank Farm

★★★B&B

Warwick Road, Stratford-upon-Avon, CV37 0NY

T:	+44 (0) 1789 292642
Bedrooms:	3
Prices:	£40.00-£48.00 per double room per night, breakfast included Cheques/cash accepted
Open:	Year round
Description:	This traditional farmhouse with exposed beams and open fires is set in beautiful countryside. Two miles from Stratford and six miles from Warwick Castle.
Facilities:	Rooms: General: P

STRATFORD-UPON-AVON

Kawartha House ★★★Guesthouse

39 Grove Road, Stratford-upon-Avon, CV37 6PB

T: +44 (0) 1789 204469
E: kawarthahouse@btopenworld.com
W: kawarthahouse.com

Bedrooms: 6

Prices: £44.00-£56.00 per double room per night, breakfast included
Debit/credit card, cheques/cash accepted

Open: Year round

Description: Comfortable guesthouse, five minutes' walk from town centre. En suite bedrooms, good food and private parking.

Facilities: Rooms:
General: P

STRATFORD-UPON-AVON

Larkrise Cottage ★★★B&B

Upper Billesley, Stratford-upon-Avon, CV37 9RA

T: +44 (0) 1789 268618
E: alanbailey17@hotmail.com
W: larkrisecottage.co.uk

Bedrooms: 2

Prices: £30.00 - £45.00 per double room per night, breakfast included
Euros accepted

Open: Year round

Description: Larkrise Cottage is located in the beautiful countryside surrounding Stratford-upon-Avon.

Facilities: Rooms:
General: P

STRATFORD-UPON-AVON

Midway ★★★Guesthouse

182 Evesham Road, Stratford-upon-Avon, CV37 9BS

T: +44 (0) 1789 204154
E: mealing@midway182.fsnet.co.uk
W: stratford-upon-avon.co.uk/midway.htm

Bedrooms: 4

Prices: £40.00-£50.00 per double room per night, breakfast included
Debit/credit card, cheques/cash, euros accepted

Open: Year round except Christmas

Description: All rooms en suite with TV, tea-/coffee-making and clock radios. Cosy, clean and homely, close to the town centre with all its many attractions.

Facilities: Rooms:
General: P

STRATFORD-UPON-AVON

Mil-Mar
★★★★Guesthouse

96 Alcester Road, Stratford-upon-Avon, CV37 9DP

T:	+44 (0) 1789 267095
E:	milmar@btinternet.com
W:	mil-mar.co.uk
Bedrooms:	6
Prices:	£40.00-£55.00 per double room per night, breakfast included Debit/credit card, cheques/cash accepted
Open:	Year round
Description:	Small, friendly guesthouse situated near to the town centre and railway station with ample parking. Tastefully decorated rooms with tea-/coffee-making facilities and colour TV. En suites available.
Facilities:	Rooms: General: **P**

STRATFORD-UPON-AVON

Minola Guesthouse
♦♦♦Guest Accommodation

25 Evesham Place, Stratford-upon-Avon, CV37 6HT

T:	+44 (0) 1789 293573
Bedrooms:	14
Prices:	£25.00 per double room per night, room only
Open:	Year round
Description:	The Minola is a late Victorian house conveniently located for the theatres and town centre. This small, friendly, family-run guesthouse has all double en suite rooms, one single room with shower en suite only and another single room.
Facilities:	Rooms: General: **P**

STRATFORD-UPON-AVON

Parkfield
★★★Guesthouse

3 Broad Walk, Stratford-upon-Avon, CV37 6HS

T:	+44 (0) 1789 293313
E:	parkfield@btinternet.com
W:	parkfieldbandb.co.uk
Bedrooms:	7
Prices:	£48.00-£50.00 per double room per night, breakfast included Debit/credit card, cheques/cash accepted, euros accepted
Open:	Year round
Description:	Victorian house with large, comfortable bedrooms. All rooms with colour TV and tea-making facilities. Quiet position, five minutes' walk from the theatre and town. Large private car park. Establishment is non-smoking. En suite rooms.
Facilities:	Rooms: General: **P**

STRATFORD-UPON-AVON

Quilt and Croissants ★★★Guesthouse

33 Evesham Place, Stratford-upon-Avon, CV37 6HT

T: +44 (0) 1789 267629
E: rooms@quilt-croissants.demon.co.uk
W: smoothhound.co.uk/hotels/quilt.html

Bedrooms: 7

Prices: £40.00-£50.00 per double room per night, breakfast included
Cheques/cash accepted

Open: Year round

Description: Family-run, comfortable Victorian guesthouse with modern facilities close to town centre, theatres and many Shakespeare properties. Convenient for racecourse.

Facilities: Rooms:
General: P

STRATFORD-UPON-AVON

Ravenhurst ★★★Guest Accommodation

2 Broad Walk, Stratford-upon-Avon, CV37 6HS

T: +44 (0) 1789 292515
E: ravaccom@waverider.co.uk
W: stratford-ravenhurst.co.uk

Bedrooms: 5

Prices: £46.00-£52.00 per double room per night, breakfast included
Debit/credit card, cheques/cash, euros accepted

Open: Year round except Christmas

Description: Quietly positioned a few minutes' walk from town centre and places of historic interest. Comfortable home, with substantial breakfast provided.

Facilities: Rooms:
General: P

STRATFORD-UPON-AVON

Salamander Guesthouse ★★★Guesthouse

40 Grove Road, Stratford-upon-Avon, CV37 6PB

T: +44 (0) 1789 205728
E: p.delin@btinternet.com
W: salamanderguesthouse.co.uk

Bedrooms: 7

Prices: £30.00-£60.00 per double room per night, breakfast included
Debit/credit card, cheques/cash, euros accepted

Open: Year round

Description: A quality family-run guesthouse in town centre within short walking distance from Stratford attractions and amenities. With own private car park/garaging on site.

Facilities: Rooms:
General: P
Leisure:

STRATFORD-UPON-AVON

The Poplars ★★★Farmhouse

Mansfield Farm, Newbold on Stour, Stratford-upon-Avon, CV37 8BZ

T: +44 (0) 1789 450540
E: juidth@poplars-farmhouse.co.uk
W: poplars-farmhouse.co.uk

Bedrooms: 3

Prices: £46.00-£60.00 per double room per night, breakfast included
Debit/credit card, cheques/cash, euros accepted

Open: Year round except Christmas

Description: Attractive en suite bedrooms enjoy views of Cotswolds in family-run beef and arable farm with stables and livery yard.

Facilities: Rooms:
General: P

STRATFORD-UPON-AVON

Virginia Lodge ★★★Guest Accommodation

12 Evesham Place, Stratford-upon-Avon, CV37 6HT

T: +44 (0) 1789 292157
E: pamela83@btinternet.com
W: virginialodge.co.uk

Bedrooms: 7

Prices: £36.00-£52.00 per double room per night, breakfast included
Debit/credit card, cheques/cash accepted

Open: Year round except Christmas

Description: Victorian guesthouse, beautifully decorated to a high standard, located in town centre. All bedrooms have own individual style. All en suite. Private car park.

Facilities: Rooms:
General: P

WARWICK

Apothecary's ♦♦♦♦Guest Accommodation

The Old Dispensary, Stratford Road, Wellesbourne, Warwick, CV35 9RN

T: +44 (0) 1789 470060
E: bandbapothecary@aol.com
W: stratford-upon-avon.co.uk/apothecarys.htm

Bedrooms: 2

Prices: £47.00-£55.00 per double room per night, breakfast included
Cheques/cash, euros accepted

Open: Year round

Description: Built in part in the mid-19thC village setting. High standard of en suite accommodation. Good quality food. Well placed for M40 and places of interest. Evening meal an optional extra.

Facilities: Rooms:
General: P

WARWICK

Church Hill Farm B&B

★★★★Farmhouse

Lighthorne, Warwick, CV35 0AR

T: +44 (0) 1926 651251
E: sue@churchhillfarm.co.uk
W: churchhillfarm.co.uk

Bedrooms: 3

Prices: £25.00-£35.00 per double room per night, breakfast included
Debit/credit card, cheques/cash, euros accepted

Open: Year round

Description: Church Hill Farm is a Grade II Listed Cruck farmhouse which dates to before the 15thC.

Facilities: Rooms:
General: P
Leisure:

SUNDERLAND

Abingdon Guesthouse

♦♦♦Guest Accommodation

5 St Georges Terrace, Roker, Sunderland, SR6 9LX

T: +44 (0) 1915 140689
E: karen@abingdonguesthouse.co.uk
W: abingdonguesthouse.co.uk

Bedrooms: 6

Prices: £38.00-£42.00 per double room per night, breakfast included
Debit/credit card, cheques/cash accepted

Open: Year round

Description: Comfortable, friendly guesthouse. Located 200 yards from seafront. Convenient for town centre and university.

Facilities: Rooms:
General: P

SUNDERLAND

Acorn Guesthouse

♦♦♦Guest Accommodation

10 Mowbray Road, Sunderland, SR2 8EN

T: +44 (0) 1915 142170
E: theacornguesthouse@hotmail.com

Bedrooms: 9

Prices: £32.00-£36.00 per double room per night, breakfast included
Debit/credit card accepted

Open: Year round

Description: Large, terraced property situated near town centre, Mowbray Park, central for stadium, theatre, Puma Centre and all local amenities. Secure parking.

Facilities: Rooms:
General: P

SUNDERLAND

Anchor Lodge ♦♦♦Guest Accommodation

16 Roker Terrace, Sunderland, SR6 9NB

T:	+44 (0) 1915 674154
E:	anchorlodge@btconnect.com
W:	anchorlodgeonline.co.uk
Bedrooms:	8
Prices:	£42.00 per double room per night, breakfast included Debit/credit card accepted
Open:	Year round except Christmas and New Year
Description:	Whether visiting family or friends, motoring, biking or sightseeing – make this your stop off point. If you are seeking a special break give us a call. Private parking. Sea views and fabulous food for breakfast.
Facilities:	Rooms: General: P

SUNDERLAND

April Guesthouse ♦♦♦♦Guest Accommodation

12 St Georges Terrace, Roker, Sunderland, SR6 9LX

T:	+44 (0) 1915 659550
E:	hilda@dickinson2772.fslife.co.uk
W:	aprilguesthouse.com
Bedrooms:	6
Prices:	£45.00 per double room per night, breakfast included Debit/credit card accepted
Open:	Year round except Christmas and New Year
Description:	Small family guesthouse, close to the sea. All rooms have en suite facilities, colour TV and tea-/coffee-making. Parking on request. Strictly non-smoking. Small refrigerator in each room.
Facilities:	Rooms: General: P

SUNDERLAND

Areldee Guesthouse ♦♦♦Guest Accommodation

18 Roker Terrace, Sunderland, SR6 9NB

T:	+44 (0) 1915 141971
E:	peter@areldeeguesthouse.freeserve.co.uk
W:	abbeyandareldeeguesthouses.co.uk
Bedrooms:	15
Prices:	£42.00-£48.00 per double room per night, breakfast included Debit/credit card, cheques/cash accepted
Open:	Year round
Description:	Family-run guesthouse on the sea front. Newly furnished en suite rooms with fabulous beach views. Breakfast may be served in your room.
Facilities:	Rooms: General: P

SUNDERLAND

Balmoral Guesthouse

★★★Guesthouse

3 Roker Terrace, Roker, Sunderland, SR6 9NB

T: +44 (0) 1915 659217
E: thebalmoral@supanet.com
W: thebalmoral.supanet.com

Bedrooms: 6

Prices: £38.00-£42.00 per double room per night, breakfast included
Debit/credit card accepted

Open: Year round

Description: The guesthouse is prominently situated on Roker seafront, within easy access of the city centre, university, Empire Theatre, Stadium of Light Football Ground and bowling alley.

Facilities: Rooms:
General: P

SUNDERLAND

Belmont Guesthouse

★★★Guesthouse

8 St Georges Terrace, Roker, Sunderland, SR6 9LX

T: +44 (0) 1915 672438
E: belmontguesthouse@freedomnames.co.uk
W: belmontguesthouse.com

Bedrooms: 6

Prices: £38.00-£42.00 per double room per night, breakfast included
Debit/credit card accepted

Open: Year round

Description: Close to the sea front and providing a friendly, relaxed atmosphere. The rooms are comfortable and the service is efficient.

Facilities: Rooms:
General: P

SUNDERLAND

Brendon Park

♦♦♦Guest Accommodation

49 Roker Park Road, Sunderland, SR6 9PL

T: +44 (0) 1915 489303
W: brendonparkguesthouse.com

Bedrooms: 5

Prices: £36.00-£50.00 per double room per night, breakfast included

Open: Seasonal opening – contact for details

Description: Small, friendly, family-run guesthouse overlooking Roker Recreation Park. Close to sea front and easy access to city centre.

Facilities: Rooms:
General: P

SUNDERLAND

Lemonfield Hotel ★★★★Guesthouse

Sea Lane, Seaburn, Sunderland, SR6 8EE

T:	+44 (0) 1915 293018
E:	gary@lemonfieldhotel.com
W:	lemonfieldhotel.com
Bedrooms:	10
Prices:	£44.00-£50.00 per double room per night, breakfast included Debit/credit card accepted
Open:	Year round except Christmas and New Year
Description:	Cream-painted hotel built in the 1930s, overlooking the sea. En suite rooms available.
Facilities:	Rooms: General: P

SUNDERLAND

Mayfield Hotel ♦♦♦Guest Accommodation

Sea Lane, Sunderland, SR6 8EE

T:	+44 (0) 1915 293345
E:	enquiries@themayfieldhotel.co.uk
W:	themayfieldhotel.co.uk
Bedrooms:	10
Prices:	£35.00-£48.00 per double room per night, breakfast included Debit/credit card, cheques/cash accepted
Open:	Seasonal opening – contact for details
Description:	Beautifully situated overlooking the sea and Seaburn Park. Walking distance to bars and restaurants. Secured car park.
Facilities:	Rooms: General: P

SUNDERLAND

Terrace Guesthouse ★★★Guesthouse

2 Roker Terrace, Roker, Sunderland, SR6 9NB

T:	+44 (0) 1915 650132
E:	thebalmoral@supanet.com
W:	thebalmoral.supanet.com
Bedrooms:	8
Prices:	£34.00-£42.00 per double room per night, breakfast included Debit/credit card accepted
Open:	Seasonal opening
Description:	Comfortable, newly refurbished guesthouse, with good standard of customer care, prominently situated on seafront, one mile from city.
Facilities:	Rooms: General: P

SUNDERLAND

The Ashborne ♦♦♦Guest Accommodation

7 St Georges Terrace, Roker, Sunderland, SR6 9LX

T:	+44 (0) 1915 653997
W:	ashborne-guesthouse.co.uk
Bedrooms:	7
Prices:	£40.00 per double room per night, breakfast included
Open:	Year round
Description:	Family-run guesthouse. All rooms have en suite, colour TV and tea-/coffee-making facilities. Central heating. Children are welcome.
Facilities:	Rooms: General:

SUNDERLAND

The Chaise Guesthouse ♦♦♦Guest Accommodation

5 Roker Terrace, Roker Seafront, Sunderland, SR6 9NB

T:	+44 (0) 1915 659218
E:	thechaise@aol.com
W:	activereservations.com/hotel/en/hotels-in-sunderland/ah-116306.html
Bedrooms:	10
Prices:	£32.00-£66.00 per double room per night, breakfast included Debit/credit card, cheques/cash accepted
Open:	Seasonal opening
Description:	Large Victorian guesthouse, seafront location. Licensed, family-run establishment. Near the town centre, Metro Centre and Beamish Museum.
Facilities:	Rooms: General: P Leisure:

SUNDERLAND

University of Sunderland ★★Campus

Clanny House, Peacock Street West, Pallion, Sunderland, SR4 6US

T:	+44 (0) 1915 153655
E:	catherine.winn@sunderland.ac.uk
Bedrooms:	84
Prices:	£22.00-£25.00 per person per night, room only Debit/credit card accepted
Open:	Year round
Description:	One hall of residence offers accommodation all year round. Other halls of residence are available throughout the summer (July-September).
Facilities:	Rooms: General: P

HIGH WYCOMBE

Trevona ★★B&B

Derehams Lane, Loudwater, High Wycombe, HP10 9RH

T: +44 (0) 1494 526715
E: ssmith4739@aol.com

Bedrooms: 2

Prices: £25.00-£55.00 per twin room per night, breakfast included

Open: Year round except Christmas and New Year
Cheques/cash accepted

Description: Two twin rooms in a family home in a quiet location. Safe parking and a heated and covered swimming pool. Close to Windsor Castle, Ascot, Henley and the River Thames.

Facilities: Rooms:
General:
Leisure:

LITTLE MARLOW

Old Barn Cottage ★★★★B&B

Old Barn Cottage, Little Marlow, Buckinghamshire, SL7 3RZ

T: +44 (0) 1628 483817
E: anthea@oldbarncottage.co.uk
W: oldbarncottage.co.uk

Bedrooms: 1

Prices: £45.00 per double room per night, breakfast included

Open: Year round except Christmas and New Year

Description: Attractive period family home in small village near Marlow. Easy access for Henley, London, Oxford, Heathrow, M4 and M40. Near to River Thames and The Thames Path. Good pub food locally.

Facilities: Rooms:
General:

MAIDENHEAD

Braywick Grange ♦♦♦♦Guest Accommodation

100 Braywick Road, Maidenhead, Berkshire, SL6 1DJ

T: +44 (0) 1628 625915
E: reception@braywickgrange.co.uk
W: braywickgrange.co.uk

Bedrooms: 3

Prices: £45.00-£60.00 per twin room per night, breakfast included
Cheques/cash, euros accepted

Open: Year round except Christmas and New Year

Description: A private house on a quiet residential road close to the town centre and the M4. Rail link to London and bus link to Heathrow.

Facilities: Rooms:
General: P
Leisure:

MAIDENHEAD

Gables End

♦♦Guest Accommodation

4 Gables Close, Maidenhead, Berkshire, Berkshire, SL6 8QD

T: +44 (0) 1628 639630
E: christablight@onetel.com

Bedrooms: 2

Prices: £42.00-£44.00 per double room per night, breakfast included
Euros accepted

Open: Year round

Description: Quiet close in residential area. Walking distance to River Thames, railway station and town centre. Motorway less than one mile away. Windsor and Eton three-four miles.

Facilities: Rooms:
General: P
Leisure:

TAPLOW

Bridge Cottage

♦♦♦Guest Accommodation

Bridge Cottage Guesthouse, Taplow, Buckinghamshire, SL6 0AR

T: +44 (0) 1628 626805
E: bridgecottagebb@aol.com
W: bridgecottageguesthouse.co.uk

Bedrooms: 6

Prices: £37.00-£60.00 per twin room per night, breakfast included

Open: Year round except Christmas and New Year

Description: Victorian cottage, near river, in large garden. Cosy, homely accommodation. Convenient for Heathrow (20 minutes), Windsor and London.

Facilities: Rooms:
General:

WINDSOR

Clarence Hotel

♦♦♦Guest Accommodation

9 Clarence Road, Windsor, SL4 5AE

T: +44 (0) 1753 864436
E: enquiries@clarence-hotel.co.uk
W: clarence-hotel.co.uk

Bedrooms: 20

Prices: £49.00-£77.00 per double room per night, breakfast included
Debit/credit card, cheques/cash accepted

Open: Year round except Christmas

Description: Hotel, close to the town centre, Windsor Castle and Eton. Licensed bar and steam sauna. Convenient for Legoland and Heathrow Airport.

Facilities: Rooms:
General: P
Leisure:

DONCASTER

The Angel Inn & Lodge ♦♦♦Guest Accommodation

Dame Lane, Misson, Doncaster, DN10 6EB

T: +44 (0) 1302 710886
E: stevedaytime@aol.com

Bedrooms: 9

Prices: £45.00 per double room per night, breakfast included

Open: Year round

Description: The Angel Inn & Lodge is set in the quiet village of Misson just four miles from the new airport at Finningley so is ideal for Park & Ride, or stay the night at our lodge and park your car for your holiday and let us take you and pick you up.

Facilities: Rooms:
General: P
Leisure:

YORK

Acres Dene Guesthouse ★★★Guest Accommodation

87 Fulford Road, York, YO10 4BD

T: +44 (0) 1904 647482
E: acresdene@tesco.net
W: acresdene.co.uk

Bedrooms: 4

Prices: £40.00-£54.00 per double room per night, breakfast included

Open: Seasonal opening – contact for details

Description: Conveniently situated on the A19 and within easy reach of the outer and inner ring roads. York's medieval city centre, the museums, and the university are just a few minutes' walk. Racecourse and McArthur Glen design outlet are two miles.

Facilities: Rooms:
General: P
Leisure:

YORK

Ascot Lodge ★★★★Guest Accommodation

112 Acomb Road, York, YO24 4EY

T: +44 (0) 1904 798234
E: info@ascotlodge.com
W: ascotlodge.com

Bedrooms: 5

Prices: £27.00-£30.00 per person per night, breakfast included

Open: Year round

Description: Beautiful Mid-Victorian guesthouse west of York. En suite accommodation. High quality double, single and family rooms. Non-smoking property. Secure, private car park.

Facilities: Rooms:
General: P

YORK

Avenue Guesthouse

★★Guest Accommodation

6 The Avenue, York, YO30 6AS

T: +44 (0) 1904 620575
E: allen@avenuegh.fsnet.co.uk
W: avenuegh.fsnet.co.uk

Bedrooms: 7

Prices: £44.00-£54.00 per double room per night, breakfast included

Open: Seasonal opening – contact for details

Description: Avenue is a Victorian house in a quiet location with easy parking and within 10 minutes' walk from the city centre and York Minster.

Facilities: Rooms:
General:

YORK

Bishopgarth Guesthouse

Rating applied for

3 Southlands Road, York, YO23 1NP

T: +44 (0) 1904 635220
E: bishopgarth@btconnect.com
W: bishopgarth.co.uk

Bedrooms: 5

Prices: £48.00-£60.00 per double room per night, breakfast included
Debit/credit card accepted

Open: Seasonal opening – contact for details

Description: Clean, comfortable, family guesthouse in a quiet location close to the centre, station and racecourse. Excellent home cooking, well-equipped rooms and friendly service guaranteed.

Facilities: Rooms:
General: P

YORK

Blossoms Hotel York

♦♦♦Guest Accommodation

28 Clifton, York, YO30 6AE

T: +44 (0) 1904 652391
E: nexus@blossomsyork.co.uk
W: blossomsyork.co.uk

Bedrooms: 7

Prices: £45.00-£95.00 per double room per night, room only
Debit/credit card accepted

Open: Year round

Description: Within easy walking distance of historic York's attractions. A warm welcome awaits at our friendly guesthouse. Car park, bar, reasonable rates.

Facilities: Rooms:
General: P

YORK

Brentwood Guesthouse ★★★★Guest Accommodation

54 Bootham Crescent, Bootham, York, YO30 7AH

T: +44 (0) 1904 636419
E: brentwoodps@aol.com
W: thebrentwood.co.uk

Bedrooms: 11

Prices: £30.00-£45.00 per double room per night, breakfast included

Open: Year round

Description: The Brentwood is a family-run guesthouse, ideally situated in the historical city of York, 10 minutes from the city centre.

Facilities: Rooms:
General:

YORK

Bull Lodge Guesthouse ★★★Guesthouse

37 Bull Lane, Lawrence Street, York, YO10 3EN

T: +44 (0) 1904 415522
E: stay@bulllodge.co.uk
W: bulllodge.co.uk

Bedrooms: 8

Prices: £42.00-£58.00 per double room per night, breakfast included
Debit/credit card accepted

Open: Seasonal opening – contact for details

Description: Modern detached guesthouse, quietly situated with private enclosed parking. Close to the city centre. Ground-floor bedroom suitable for the elderly or accompanied handicapped.

Facilities: Rooms:
General: P

YORK

Chelmsford Place ♦♦♦Guest Accommodation

85 Fulford Road, York, YO10 4BD

T: +44 (0) 1904 624491
E: chelmsfordplace@btinternet.com
W: chelmsfordplace.co.uk

Bedrooms: 6

Prices: £42.00-£64.00 per double room per night, breakfast included
Debit/credit card, euros accepted

Open: Seasonal opening – closed New Year

Description: Quiet, fully restored, friendly-run guesthouse offering accommodation at a moderate price. Ten minutes' walk from York centre.

Facilities: Rooms:
General: P

YORK

Dalescroft Guesthouse ♦♦♦Guest Accommodation

10 Southlands Road, York, YO23 1NP

T: +44 (0) 1904 626801
W: dalescroft-york.co.uk

Bedrooms: 5

Prices: £40.00-£70.00 per double room per night, breakfast included
Debit/credit card accepted

Open: Year round

Description: Comfortable, family-run guesthouse close to the city centre and racecourse. Full English breakfast. En suite rooms available. Totally non-smoking.

Facilities: Rooms:
General:

YORK

Farthings Guesthouse ★★★★Guesthouse

5 Nunthorpe Avenue, York, YO23 1PF

T: +44 (0) 1904 653545
E: stay@farthingsyork.co.uk
W: farthingsyork.co.uk

Bedrooms: 9

Prices: £48.00-£58.00 per double room per night, breakfast included
Debit/credit card accepted

Open: Year round

Description: Family-run Victorian guesthouse in quiet cul-de-sac close to centre. Non-smoking. On-street parking. English and continental breakfast.

Facilities: Rooms:
General: P

YORK

Foss Bank Guesthouse ♦♦♦Guest Accommodation

16 Huntington Road, York, YO31 8RB

T: +44 (0) 1904 635548
E: please@call.above.number.uk
W: fossbank.co.uk

Bedrooms: 5

Prices: £48.00-£58.00 per double room per night, breakfast included
Euros accepted

Open: Seasonal opening – contact for details

Description: Small Victorian guesthouse overlooking the river Foss. Ten minutes' walk to York Minster. Non-smoking property throughout. Private car park.

Facilities: Rooms:
General: P

YORK

Friars Rest Guesthouse

81 Fulford Road, York, YO10 4BD

T: +44 (0) 1904 629823
E: friarsrest@btinternet.com
W: friarsrest.co.uk

Bedrooms: 7

Prices: £40.00-£66.00 per double room per night, breakfast included
Debit/credit card accepted

Open: Year round

Description: Friars Rest offers seven en suite comfortable bedrooms, all are well furnished, with colour TV, tea-/coffee-making facilities and radio alarm. We have a free private car park and on-road parking permits.

Facilities: Rooms:
General: P

YORK

Glade Farm ♦♦♦♦Guest Accommodation

Riccall Road, Escrick, York, YO19 6ED

T: +44 (0) 1904 728098
E: victorialeaf@hotmail.com

Bedrooms: 2

Prices: £45.00 per double room per night, breakfast included

Open: Seasonal opening – contact for details

Description: Just eight miles from York on the A19, 300-acre arable farm offers a warm family welcome. TV, tea-/coffee-making facilities, guest lounge.

Facilities: Rooms:
General: P
Leisure:

YORK

Greenside ★★Guesthouse

124 Clifton, York, YO30 6BQ

T: +44 (0) 1904 623631
E: greenside@amserve.com
W: greensideguesthouse.co.uk

Bedrooms: 8

Prices: £40.00 per double room per night, breakfast included
Euros accepted

Open: Year round

Description: Fronted onto Clifton Green, the owner-run guesthouse is ideally situated for all of York's attractions. Offers all facilities for guests in a homely atmosphere. Licensed.

Facilities: Rooms:
General: P

YORK

Holgate Bridge Hotel ♦♦♦Guest Accommodation

106-108 Holgate Road, York, YO24 4BB

T: +44 (0) 1904 635971
E: info@holgatebridge.co.uk
W: holgatebridge.co.uk

Bedrooms: 13

Prices: £30.00-£70.80 per double room per night, breakfast included
Debit/credit card, euros accepted

Open: Seasonal opening – contact for details

Description: The Holgate Bridge is a B&B establishment located in York. It is ideally situated for sightseeing, close to the centre of York, only a short walk from Micklegate Bar, the nearest gateway into the heart of the city.

Facilities: Rooms:
General: P

YORK

Minster View Guesthouse Rating applied for

2 Grosvenor Terrace, York, YO30 7AJ

T: +44 (0) 1904 655034
E: minsterview@amserve.com

Bedrooms: 3

Prices: £45.00-£50.00 per double room per night, breakfast included

Open: Year round

Description: Minster View is situated in a quiet position overlooking parks to the west of the Minster, its proximity to the city centre allows residents immediate pedestrian access to the many pleasures of York. Classically refurbished to its original look.

Facilities: Rooms:
General: P

YORK

Olga's Licensed Guesthouse ★★★Guesthouse

12 Wenlock Terrace, Fulford Road, York, YO10 4DU

T: +44 (0) 1904 641456
E: olgasguesthouseyork@tiscali.co.uk
W: olgas-guesthouse-york.co.uk

Bedrooms: 10

Prices: £40.00-£70.00 per double room per night, breakfast included

Open: Year round

Description: Specially built for officers of the cavalry in the 1800s. A quiescent locale, congenial company, cop acetic cuisine and superlative service. Close proximity to all major attractions, university and Fulford Golf Course.

Facilities: Rooms:
General: P
Leisure:

YORK

Orillia House
★★★★Guest Accommodation

89 The Village, Stockton on the Forest, York, YO32 9UP

T: +44 (0) 1904 400600
E: info@orilliahouse.co.uk
W: orilliahouse.co.uk

Bedrooms: 8

Prices: £30.00-£30.00 per double room per night, breakfast included
Debit/credit card accepted

Open: Seasonal opening – contact for details

Description: Warm welcome awaits you in this 300-year-old house of charm and character. Situated opposite the church, three miles north east of York.

Facilities: Rooms:
General: P
Leisure:

YORK

Papillon Hotel
★★Guesthouse

43 Gillygate, York, YO31 7EA

T: +44 (0) 1904 636505
E: papillonhotel@btinternet.com
W: btinternet.com/~papillonhotel

Bedrooms: 8

Prices: £48.00-£56.00 per double room per night, breakfast included
Debit/credit card accepted

Open: Seasonal opening – closed Christmas

Description: Papillon is a small, friendly, family-run B&B, three minutes' walk from York Minster. Limited car parking available. Non-smoking establishment.

Facilities: Rooms:
General: P

YORK

Romley House
★★★Guest Accommodation

2 Millfield Road, York, YO23 1NQ

T: +44 (0) 1904 652822
E: info@romleyhouse.co.uk
W: romleyhouse.co.uk

Bedrooms: 6

Prices: £42.00-£56.00 per double room per night, breakfast included

Open: Seasonal opening – closed Christmas

Description: Friendly, family-run, licensed guesthouse, 10 minutes' walk from York city centre.

Facilities: Rooms:
General: P
Leisure:

YORK

Rush Farm

♦♦♦Guest Accommodation

York Road, York, YO19 6HQ

T:	+44 (0) 1904 728459
E:	david@rushfarm.co.uk
W:	rushfarm.fsnet.co.uk
Bedrooms:	5
Prices:	£45.00-£60.00 per double room per night, breakfast included Debit/credit card accepted
Open:	Seasonal opening – contact for details
Description:	Small holding with open views over farmland. Convenient to many places of interest.
Facilities:	Rooms: General: P Leisure:

YORK

South Newlands Farm

★★★B&B

Selby Road, Riccall, York, YO19 6QR

T:	+44 (0) 1757 248203
E:	southnewlandsfarm@yahoo.co.uk
Bedrooms:	2
Prices:	£40.00-£50.00 per double room per night, breakfast included Debit/credit card, euros accepted
Open:	Seasonal opening Closed New Year
Description:	All guests receive the warmest of welcomes and the best of traditional Yorkshire hospitality. Food is fresh and plentiful and the kettle is always on the boil. Well located for the park and ride system, giving easy access to the centre of the city.
Facilities:	Rooms: General: P Leisure:

YORK

Staymor Guesthouse

★★★★Guesthouse

2 Southlands Road, York, YO23 1NP

T:	+44 (0) 1904 626935
E:	kathwilson@lineone.net
W:	staymorguesthouse.com
Bedrooms:	5
Prices:	£40.00-£60.00 per double room per night, breakfast included Debit/credit card accepted
Open:	Seasonal opening – contact for details
Description:	Traditional guesthouse with emphasis on food and comfort. Close to city centre. Fire certificate.
Facilities:	Rooms: General: P

YORK

Sycamore Guesthouse ♦♦♦Guest Accommodation

19 Sycamore Place, York, YO30 7DW

T: +44 (0) 1904 624712
E: mail@thesycamore.co.uk
W: thesycamore.co.uk

Bedrooms: 6

Prices: £46.00-£68.00 per double room per night, breakfast included

Open: Seasonal opening – closed Christmas

Description: Family-run guesthouse in a quiet cul-de-sac. Close to the river, city centre, York Minster and museums.

Facilities: Rooms:
General: **P**
Leisure:

YORK

York Backpackers Rating applied for

88-90 Micklegate, York, YO1 6JX

T: +44 (0) 1904 627720
E: mail@yorkbackpackers.co.uk
W: yorkbackpackers.co.uk

Dormitories: 2

Prices: £9.00-£17.50 per person per night, breakfast included
Debit/credit card, euros accepted

Open: Seasonal Opening – contact for details

Description: Ideal budget accommodation, catering for single travellers up to groups of 125 and ages 1 to 100.

Facilities: Rooms:
General:
Leisure: